MODERN WORLD NATIONS

MODERN WORLD NATIONS

Kazakhstan

Zoran Pavlović

Series Consulting Editor

Charles F. Gritzner

South Dakota State University

CHELSEA HOUSE

PUBLISHERS

A Haights Cross Communications Company

Philadelphia

Frontispiece: Flag of Kazakhstan

Cover: Horseback riders hunting with golden eagles.

CHELSEA HOUSE PUBLISHERS

VP, NEW PRODUCT DEVELOPMENT Sally Cheney
DIRECTOR OF PRODUCTION Kim Shinners
CREATIVE MANAGER Takeshi Takahashi
MANUFACTURING MANAGER Diann Grasse

Staff for KAZAKHSTAN

EXECUTIVE EDITOR Lee Marcott
PRODUCTION EDITOR Jaimie Winkler
PICTURE RESEARCHER 21st Century Publishing and Communications, Inc.
SERIES DESIGNER Takeshi Takahashi
COVER DESIGNER Keith Trego
LAYOUT 21st Century Publishing and Communications, Inc.

A Haights Cross Communications Company

http://www.chelseahouse.com

First Printing

1 3 5 7 9 8 6 4 2

Library of Congress Cataloging-in-Publication Data

Pavlovic´, Zoran.
   Kazakhstan / by Zoran "Zok" Pavlovic´.
      p. cm.
Includes index.
   ISBN 0-7910-7231-2
   1. Kazakhstan—Juvenile literature. I. Title.
DK903 .P38 2003
958.45—dc21

2002153508

Table of Contents

Kazakhstan

Kazakhstan is a landlocked country that is far from most of the world's major population centers. Despite these disadvantages, the land is one of stunning contrasts, as seen in this view of eastern Kazakhstan's snow-capped mountains rising in the distance behind the flat, arid plains.

1

Introducing Kazakhstan

O ccupying an area of more than 1 million square miles (2.6 million square kilometers), Kazakhstan is the world's ninth-largest country. If superimposed over the United States, it would cover almost all the territory between the Mississippi River and the Atlantic Coast, yet most Americans possess a blank "mental map" of this sprawling Central Asian giant. Its location, physical landscapes, people and their way of life, and history remain a mystery to many. This book profiles this fascinating country in an effort to fill in the reader's mental map with many of the details that make Kazakhstan such a unique place on the global stage.

Kazakhstan is the largest of five Central Asian countries that gained their independence with the fall of the Union of Soviet Socialist Republics (USSR), better known as the Soviet Union, in the early 1990s. Before achieving its independence in December 1991,

Kazakhstan had been an Autonomous Socialist Republic within the USSR for almost 70 years. The other four former Soviet republics in Central Asia are Uzbekistan, Turkmenistan, Kyrgyzstan, and Tajikistan. These four together, however, occupy an area smaller than that of Kazakhstan.

Because of its strategic geographic location, enormous size, and rising regional importance, the somewhat remote Kazakhstan has nevertheless earned a position among major world nations.

During the autumn of 2001, following the September 11 terrorist attacks in New York City and Washington, D.C., the United States sent military forces to areas in Central Asia to gain proximity to Afghanistan, which it believed was harboring the organizations responsible for the attacks. American troops were deployed in Uzbekistan, Tajikistan, and Kyrgyzstan. Kazakhstan also cooperated with the United States in its efforts, and, because of the resulting media attention to these events, what had been a forgotten part of the world suddenly became a focus of attention. Press coverage of the former Soviet territory brought Americans more information about Kazakhstan and its neighbors in a single year than it had during the preceding half-century. This serves as a splendid reminder of how important an understanding of geography is in an increasing global community: any place in the world can suddenly become extremely important!

During the Cold War (ideological conflict between the United States and the USSR) in the mid- to late-twentieth century, the Eastern European regions located behind what British prime minister Winston Churchill called the "Iron Curtain" (ideological border demarcating Soviet-controlled territories from non-Soviet nations in Europe) received little attention in American secondary or higher education text-books. As a result, in most Americans' minds, Eastern Europe and the Soviet portions of northern Asia were little more than a vast, red-colored wilderness ("Red" is the term used to refer to the Communist Party, which was predominant in the USSR, and thus the color was often used to characterize this part of the world). Its inhabitants were simply called "Russians," even though Russia was just one of the 15 republics in the USSR, and ethnic Russians did not even represent the absolute majority of the population.

In the United States, references to Kazakhstan used to be quite negative. One reason for our lack of knowledge was the mass of invalid information about the region that was published throughout the years. Some of the problem stemmed from the fact that very little factual information was known about the USSR and its republics during the Cold War era. It was thus not a place where "good things happened." Three events that helped Americans develop this negative mental image of Kazakhstan included: its role as the Soviet Union's nuclear weapons testing center; it was the destination for all ethnic groups relocated by Soviet leader Joseph Stalin because they collaborated with the enemy (Germany and its allies) during World War II; and the environmental degradation of the Aral Sea (the largest part of which is within the country's borders). Rarely had Kazakhstan been mentioned in a positive light, even though the republic's history includes more uplifting aspects. Subsequent chapters will discuss these events in Kazakhstan's development in more detail.

Few people realized that behind the red color was hidden one of the most complex and interesting regions in the world. After Kazakhstan and neighboring republics achieved their independence in 1991, the Western world finally began to learn more about them. While stereotype-filled information about Central Asians still dominates in many classrooms, slowly but surely more accurate information is becoming available on this complex region. This book represents a fresh attempt to widen our knowledge about contemporary Kazakhstan by presenting a comprehensive summary of information currently available.

Located in the heart of Asia, Kazakhstan shares its border

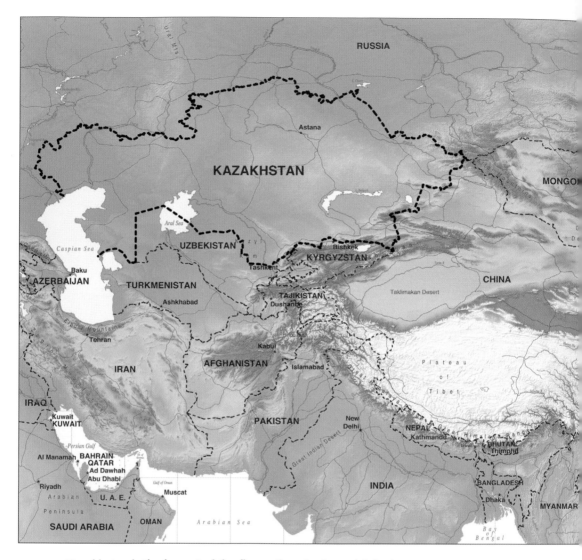

Kazakhstan is the largest of the five nations in Central Asia that were part of the Soviet Union before they won their independence in 1991. Adjacent to Russia and China, Kazakhstan is in a location that was considered strategic during conflicts of the twentieth century.

with some of the world's largest and most influential countries. They include the world's largest country, Russia, on the north and the fourth-largest, China, on the east and southeast. Its southern neighbors are, from west to east, Turkmenistan,

Uzbekistan, and Kyrgyzstan. The Caspian Sea forms much of its western boundary.

Despite its huge area, Kazakhstan is a landlocked country. Lack of access to the global sea (oceans) poses a major obstacle to economic development. Isolated from major trade routes in the past, Kazakhstan was a victim of, and continues to suffer from, the effects of its remote location. Today, however, the country is attempting to combine geopolitical realities based on its location with the exploitation of its abundant natural resources in hope of becoming a significant political and economic factor in the region.

Kazakhstan faces two major challenges on the path to development: it must develop both a strong democratic government and a free-market economy. Both must be free from the widespread corruption that poses a huge obstacle to achieving stability in either area. Kazakh society is working to implement democratic principles and a market economy after many decades of rule by an authoritarian regime that allowed neither.

In the following pages you will journey through the country of Kazakhstan. You will travel its vast natural landscapes in search of the problems and prospects they offer. You will mingle with the country's people and wander through the corridors of time as the country's history takes shape. Finally, you will experience many revealing views of Kazakhstan's political and economic activity, its cities and regions, and its prospects for the future.

To understand present-day Kazakhstan, you must understand its past. How did this land develop from a place inhabited by various bands of nomadic Turkic tribes that for countless centuries wandered across the region's steppes and deserts, into a modern nation of people who entered the twenty-first century eager to face its many opportunities and challenges? Let your journey into this once isolated and little-known area of the world begin; it is a fascinating land that deserves to be discovered.

The Tian Shan Mountains form much of Kazakhstan's border with China and Krygyzstan. Although the lower areas around these mountains are extremely dry, the mountains themselves contain lush vegetation.

Physical Landscapes

K azakhstan's physical geography is dominated by two primary factors: its area and location. Because of its huge size— 1.48 million square miles (2.6 million square kilometers)— the country has a considerable variety of land features. Mountains along the southeastern border tower to nearly 23,000 feet (7,000 meters); yet in the west, in a depression north of the Caspian Sea, the elevation plunges to more than 400 feet (122 meters) below sea level. In the country's midlatitude continental interior, location contributes to a climate marked by general aridity, hot summers, and cold winters.

Although Kazakhstan is not connected to any of the world's oceans, the country does have hundreds of miles of shoreline and beaches. In the west, it borders the world's largest lake, the Caspian Sea (geographers recognize the water body as a lake, but its large area gives the impression of its being a sea).

Kazakhstan is physically a beautiful country, particularly to those who are attracted to desert landscapes. A considerable variety of natural features, however, can be found to satisfy even the pickiest travelers. In this chapter, attention will be focused on those physical features and conditions that are of greatest importance to the country and its people.

Kazakhstan presents both challenges and opportunities for land use and economic development. The Kazakh people have developed a culture (way of life) that is finely tuned to the natural environments that they occupy. In following chapters you will learn, for example, how Russian imperialism and colonization were organized to follow the physical landscape. This policy resulted in the current distribution of settlement in the country.

A CONTINENTAL LOCATION

Kazakhstan occupies a large area in the interior of the Eurasian landmass. Because of its central position, nearly all of the country is at least 1,550 miles (2,495 kilometers) from the closest ocean. In fact, the so-called world pole—the point of Earth's land surface located the greatest distance from an ocean—is in the Trans-Ili Alatay Mountains in the country's eastern region.

It is with good reason that Kazakhstan and its neighbors are called Central Asian countries. They are clustered in the very heart of the huge Eurasian landmass and Asia proper. Only Kazakhstan and its larger northern neighbor, Russia, span the thousands of miles between China and Europe.

BORDERS

The western border of modern Kazakhstan extends westward to the delta of the Volga River, the longest river in both Europe and Russia. The southern ridges of the Ural Mountains, the ancient and traditional border between Europe and Asia, extend into northwestern Kazakhstan. (The Urals form a natural division between Russia's European provinces and Siberia.) Kazakhstan and Russia share one of the world's longest boundaries—4,253 miles (6,846 kilometers) in length—that begins just a few miles from Mongolia and reaches not far from the Russian cities of Astrakhan and Volgograd (previously known as Stalingrad). Most of the boundary runs through southern Siberia and the Turanian Lowlands.

The eastern border with China and southeastern border with Kyrgyzstan mostly follow the high Tian Shan and western Altai mountain ranges. The southwestern border with Uzbekistan and Turkmenistan passes almost completely through an arid landscape. Here, the parched surfaces of the Kyzyl Kum and Kara Kum (*Kum* means desert) are broken only by the rapidly vanishing waters of the Aral Sea. All together, Kazakhstan stretches over 1,900 miles (3,060 kilometers) from east to west and 1,200 miles (1,930 kilometers) from north to south.

LANDFORMS

Rolling lowland plains are the dominant landform feature of Kazakhstan. However, more than 23,000 feet (7,000 meters) separate the country's highest and lowest points of elevation. In the southeastern corner, near the border with Kyrgyzstan, snow-clad Khan-Thengri peak soars to an elevation of 22,958 feet (6,998 meters). In the west, at Karagiye in the Caspian depression (see next paragraph), the elevation drops to 433 feet (132 meters) below sea level.

The dominant land feature of western Kazakhstan is the huge depression occupied by the Caspian Sea. The region includes the Syrt and Turanian lowlands. The sea itself occupies the lowest part of the depression, which originally was filled with water during the last Ice Age. Since the end of the Ice Age some 10,000 years ago, the Caspian has been shrinking. It is in an area that receives little precipitation, and evaporation is high because of the desert heat. Only one large river (the Volga) flows into the sea. The result of this shrinkage is the expansion of a desert landscape covered with sand and clay, serving as reminders that the now dry land was once a seabed.

Kazakhstan occupies a large area in the interior of the Eurasian landmass. This huge country has an area of 1.48 million square miles (2.6 million square kilometers). Nearly all of the country is over 1,500 miles (2,495 kilometers) from the closest ocean, although it does border the world's largest lake, the Caspian Sea. The landlocked character of the country has had a strong impact on its history.

Kazakhstan has about 900 miles (1,448 kilometers) of coastline along the Caspian Sea. Sandstone outcrops that have been scoured, shaped, and reshaped by the erosive action of windblown sand are common features of the region.

North of the Caspian depression, the Ural Mountains reach a short distance into Kazakhstan's northwestern region. The area is one of heavily eroded hills and low mountains. Traveling about 375 miles (600 kilometers) east from the Caspian Sea, one reaches another large body of water, the Aral Sea. It occupies a depression in the Turanian Lowland. This low-lying plain covers most of west-central Kazakhstan. It is mainly an arid to semiarid landscape that gradually increases in elevation toward the north and east.

Kazakhstan's south-central border area is one of deserts interrupted by occasional green oases. The largest sandy desert is Kyzyl Kum, which continues southward into Uzbekistan. The country's most important river is the Syr Darya. This "exotic stream" (a river that flows throughout the year in a desert environment), flows northward from the high, snow-covered mountains of Kyrgyzstan. It forms a large oasis, with thousands of acres of irrigated crops, before its then meager flow drains into the Aral Sea. A landscape composed mainly of arid lowlands continues from the Aral Sea eastward to Lake Balkhash (Balqash). Balkhash, although quite large in area, is very shallow, with a depth averaging perhaps 15 feet (5 meters). The lake occupies a basin of interior drainage. With no outflow, much of its water is saline. Where several small rivers flow into the lake, however, the water is fresh. This explains the strange occurrence of a lake that is comprised of both fresh water and salt water!

Southeastern Kazakhstan is a land of high, rugged, heavily glaciated mountains. Several ranges, including the Kirgiz, Tian Shan, and Altai, reach into the country. These highlands are home to an estimated 200,000 glaciers. They vary in size, but most of the glaciers are small, with an area of no more than half a square mile (1 square kilometer). A few glaciers are as large as 4 square miles (10 square kilometers).

The northeastern one-third of Kazakhstan is an area of hills, plateaus, and low mountains. Ice Age glaciers scoured basins now occupied by lakes that dot the landscape.

Kazakhstan's soils vary widely in quality and characteristics. Approximately 12 percent of Kazakhstan has soils that are suitable for agriculture. In much of the western, southern, and central portions of the country, soils are alkaline, sandy, and often saline—very poorly suited for agriculture. In the eastern and southeastern upland areas, soil—where present—is of better quality, presenting an opportunity for high-yield farming.

Most of Kazakhstan's more than 7,000 streams flow into lakes, or simply evaporate in the parched desert. Very little stream water leaves the country. Only three major rivers—the Irtysh, Ishim, and Tobol—flow northward to join larger Russian rivers that ultimately drain into the Arctic Ocean.

WEATHER AND CLIMATE

Arid deserts and semiarid steppe (short) grasslands dominate Kazakhstan's landscapes. Scientists agree that because of unwise agricultural policies followed during the long era of Soviet control, the country's desert landscapes will continue to expand. The creation of desert conditions by unwise human practices such as overgrazing or the farming of marginal land is called desertification. Desertification most frequently occurs in areas of semiarid (dry continental) climates. If grasslands continue to be overgrazed and farmland continues to be eaten away by wind and water erosion, it is estimated that as much as 60 percent of Kazakhstan will be covered by desert in the next few decades. Currently, some 44 percent of Kazakhstan is classified as desert. This is just one example of the many ways in which climate is critical to both the physical and cultural geography of the country.

Weather and climate are the single most important elements of physical geography. Temperature and moisture are the primary influences on natural vegetation, animal habitat, soil formation, and surface water features. Each of these, in turn, represents the natural resource base that is available to the human population. These are the elements upon which we depend for our very survival.

Weather is defined as the daily condition of the atmosphere; climate is the long-term average condition of the day-to-day weather. Kazakhstan's climate is influenced by several key factors: distance from the sea, continental location, and elevation. The country's distance from the sea contributes to its isolation from maritime weather influence, in particular from any oceanic source of atmospheric moisture. As a result, precipitation is sparse throughout nearly all of the country. In the bone-dry west, only rarely do moisture-bearing air masses penetrate the area, bringing temporary relief to an otherwise parched landscape.

Kazakhstan's continental midlatitude location contributes to its temperature extremes as well, including hot summers and cold winters. Because temperatures decrease with increased elevation, temperatures throughout much of the country are strongly influenced by this control. Mountains also influence precipitation, often being considerably wetter than surrounding lowlands. And because of the lower temperatures at higher elevations, there is less loss of moisture from evaporation.

Kazakhstan falls within three climatic zones: arid (desert), dry continental (steppe), and highland (conditions varying with elevation and exposure to the sun). Arid conditions, with parched desert landscapes, characterize 40 to 50 percent of the country. Here, annual precipitation amounts to less than 10 inches (25 centimeters) and all farmland must be irrigated. Another roughly 40 percent of the country falls within a broad belt of dry continental climate that spans much of Central Asia. Here, 10 to 20 inches (25 to 50 centimeters) of moisture is adequate to support the steppe grasslands that make excellent pasture, and some dry farming (farming without use of irrigation) is possible. Conditions are very similar to those of western North and South Dakota and Montana east of the Rocky Mountains. Finally, in the mountainous regions, temperature and moisture can vary greatly over very short horizontal distances. Vertical distance, or elevation, is the primary control of temperature, moisture, and vegetation cover. Some areas receive up to 30 inches (800 millimeters) of precipitation a year, most of which falls as snow.

Since there is no large water body to moderate temperatures, Kazakhstan is subject to drastic temperature variations during the year. Summers are hot, with temperatures often climbing over 90° F (32° C) throughout much of the country and soaring as high as 110° F (43° C) in the southwestern deserts. Winter temperatures often fall well below zero (−18° C). During the winter, when frigid, high-pressure Siberian air masses penetrate the region, temperatures in the north can drop to 50° F below zero (−46° C). The continental climate allows the stabilization of air masses over Kazakhstan for long periods of time. This condition often provides for clear days with a lot of sun. The average annual number of sunny days for most of Kazakhstan is 200.

VEGETATION AND WILDLIFE

Climatic zones with different amounts of precipitation host different species of flora (plant life) and fauna (animal life). In western Kazakhstan, where a lack of significant precipitation exists, species have had to adapt to life in an arid environment with very high air and surface temperatures during the summer months. In the mountains and the country's northern areas, the situation is quite different. There, species have had to adapt to conditions of extreme cold that occur during the long winter months. Very little of Kazakhstan is forested. Woodlands, found mainly in the cooler, wetter mountainous areas, cover only about 4 percent of the country's total land area. There is almost no woodland whatsoever in the western desert and steppe region.

The desert surface is dominated, where plants exist at all, by scattered xerophytic (drought-resistant) plant species. Most are small and scattered across the desert floor, often in clumps. Such plants are well adapted to desert conditions. Very small leaves and very long root systems are two of many characteristics that help such desert plants survive.

Large areas of Kazakhstan, especially in the west, are composed of arid desert landscape. In these dry regions with virtually no vegetation, not even hardy trees or shrubs can survive.

Desert life centers on those few areas where precious water supplies create an oasis environment (an oasis is any place in a desert region where good water is available by any means). In the desert, larger plants and trees are found only in these oasis areas. Irrigated farming and pasture herding of livestock are the primary economic activities found in these widely scattered islands of green in a sea of desert yellow and brown.

In the semiarid regions, precipitation is adequate to support a short-grass ecosystem called steppe. Here, too, life can be very difficult. For centuries, this has been home to nomadic peoples whose culture is fine-tuned to those challenges posed by the natural environment. Nomads are people who do not have a fixed place of residence. Rather, they follow their grazing herds.

Rather than random wandering, nomads follow a very rigid schedule and route of migration. They know that staying in one place too long will cause the grassland to be ruined by overgrazing. Basically, their route is determined by seasonal variations in available food and water for their herds in each location. For example, many nomads practice *transhumance,* by which they herd their livestock into cooler, wetter uplands during the summer months and back onto the lowland plains during the winter. Today, pastoral nomadism is a vanishing way of life. As has happened throughout the steppe region of the United States, waving fields of grain crops (particularly wheat) have replaced much of the native steppe grasslands.

Southern Kazakhstan is home to wormwood, a strong-smelling plant that produces a bitter-tasting oil used in making absinthe (a liqueur). As a matter of fact, more than 500 native plant species grow only in Kazakhstan. Tree species such as cedar, larch, and spruce can be found in the mountains, especially at higher elevations. In general, Kazakhstan is home to thousands of plant species and hundreds of different forms of animal life. Open country sparsely populated with humans creates an environment that is ideal for the development of wildlife.

While in many parts of the world conservationists have problems preserving animal species from extinction, in Kazakhstan many of them are increasing in number. The wolf population, for example, has increased in size over time to over 125,000 animals. In fact, during recent years, many farmers have complained that wolves are destroying their livestock. Wildcats, boars, goats, bears, deer, and the famous snow leopard, together with many bird species, including the golden eagle, live in the Kazakhstan mountains. Desert fauna is more sparse than that of the steppes and mountains but includes scattered populations of such large animals as the famous Bukhara deer, gazelles, and wild boars. Most desert wildlife, however, is small in size. Like desert flora, all animals must be well adapted to desert conditions.

An estimated 150 species of fish inhabit Kazakhstan's several thousand lakes. The most sought-after are sturgeon, roach, herring, trout, perch, and carp. Because of ineffective environmental policies leading to overfishing, many lakes and rivers have experienced a decline in fish populations. The most significant environmental degradation and loss of fish resources has happened in the Aral Sea. This water body was once a major source of fish. Today, because of pollution and shrinkage of the lake itself, most of the fish species have died out. The country is attempting to restore the quality and quantity of water in the Aral Sea, but it will take decades to bring the water and fish production back to a satisfactory level. (See page 27 for more information on this issue.)

Kazakhstan has nine nature reserves, developed in an attempt to preserve some of the country's natural treasures. The reserve system is a continuation of environmental decisions first implemented by the Soviet Union beginning in the 1920s. The goal is to allow nature to restore itself to its earlier natural form. Kazakhstan's people take great pride in these reserves and their beauty. The mountains of south Kazakhstan are home to two of the reserves, Aksu-Jabagli and Almaty. Aksu-Jabagli was founded in 1927 and is a UNESCO (United Nations Educational, Scientific, and Cultural Organization) biosphere reserve. The breathtaking canyon of the Aksu River is an erosion-caused scar cut some 1,500 feet (457 meters) deep and is home to hundreds of species of birds, insects, and animals and some 1,300 species of plants. Almaty reserve is located in the southern Tian Shan Mountains. It is known for the great variety of natural features that are being preserved, ranging from snow-capped mountain peaks and glaciers, to 450-foot (15-meter)-high, crescent-shaped barchan sand dunes. Among its many animal species are rare snow leopards. The reserve is perhaps best known for its remarkable "singing sands," called so because they produce an organ-like sound when the wind is blowing from the west, or when people walk over their surface.

Western Kazakhstan also has several reserves. The Ustiurt reserve is located in the Karagie depression 433 feet (132 meters) below sea level. Desert landscapes and sizzling hot temperatures are major characteristics of this reserve, which is the country's largest. Barsa Kelmes reserve is located on an island in the Aral Sea. The name, translated, means, "land of no return." The island is home to the kulan, the world's rarest hoofed animal. Other reserves include the Marakol and West Altai reserves, both located in the Altai Mountains of eastern Kazakhstan.

The Kurgaldjino reserve, located in central Kazakhstan, also is of international importance. It preserves natural feather-grass steppe and is recognized as a place of exceptional natural beauty. The reserve also is home to the world's most northerly settlement of nesting pink flamingos. The Naurzum reserve in northern Kazakhstan protects a large pine forest and many species of animals. It is particularly noted for its rare bird species, including white herons, hisser swans, grave eagles, and jack-bustards. Finally, Bayan-Aul National Park, often called the "Museum of Nature," is located in central Kazakhstan. The park is an oasis of trees located on a small area of highland surrounded by steppe-covered plains.

ENVIRONMENTAL CONCERNS

During recent decades, Kazakhstan has experienced several major environmental problems that have had a very negative effect on both humans and the environment. Unlike some natural hazards over which humans have little if any control, these disasters were of human origin. They were caused by irresponsible human use of the natural environment and weapons and scientific tests conducted with little concern for human or environmental safety. Today, many agencies, both domestic and international, are searching for solutions to Kazakhstan's environmental problems. It is obvious, however, that it will take many decades, even centuries, before the country's most serious problems can be reversed.

One of the most significant challenges in this area is that posed by the Aral Sea. This body of water is probably one of the world's worst (and best) examples of how the irresponsible use of natural resources can affect both the environment and human lives. The sea once covered an area of 26,250 square miles (68,000 square kilometers), roughly the size of West Virginia. Today, it has shrunk to only one-third its pre-1960 size and threatens to disappear completely, leaving only a dusty desert surface. Under natural conditions, two large rivers maintained the water level in the Aral Sea. The Amu Darya and Syr Darya have their headwaters in high mountains located hundreds of miles south of Kazakhstan. The streams flow through desert landscapes in Uzbekistan and Turkmenistan and ultimately empty into the Aral Sea. In Uzbekistan, however, policymakers diverted millions of cubic feet of water from the rivers to irrigate cotton fields. Water for irrigation was also diverted to Turkmenistan through a 660-mile (1200-kilometer)-long canal. These diversions, coupled with a very high loss of water from evaporation, have combined to make the fate of the Aral Sea a huge environmental problem confronting Kazakhstan today. Much like the situation facing the Rio Grande and Colorado Rivers, shared by the United States and Mexico, little if any water is left by the time the streams reach the sea. Finally, dams built in Kyrgystan to provide electricity and water for irrigation also cause a decrease in available water discharge.

With little coordination, international cooperation, or environmental resource control, the total water discharge into the Aral Sea became insufficient to preserve the lake's original size. In the late 1980s, it began to shrink rapidly. Two important fishing ports in the Aral Sea, Aralsk in Kazakhstan and Moynak in Uzbekistan, became deserts. The sea once had a fish population that included 24 different species. Fishing and fish processing industries in the region once employed 60,000 workers. As the water level declined, so the did fishing industry, until today both are all but gone. Since what once was a thriving lake is now

A large portion of the Aral Sea falls within the borders of Kazakhstan. Once the fourth-largest lake in the world, the Aral Sea has been shrinking in recent years due to the increasing use of its waters for irrigating crops. This photograph, taken from space, shows the reduced area of the Aral Sea, which is now one-third of its pre-1960s size.

rapidly turning into desert, people already are beginning to call the Aral Sea the Aral Kum (desert).

In addition to fish species reduction, severe health problems are afflicting the local human population as a result of pollution around the lake. Scientists blame the heavy use of pesticides and fertilizers in agricultural production for the high cancer and infant mortality rates.

The Semipalatinsk nuclear testing center is another area of primary environmental concern. For three decades, with little concern for the environment or well-being of the local population, Soviet nuclear engineers tested various types of nuclear weapons in northeastern Kazakhstan's Semipalatinsk oblast (province), resulting in 470 nuclear explosions during a 30-year period. Since nuclear testing was always covered in a shroud of secrecy, inhabitants of neighboring towns and villages were never informed about the details of the experiments. Tests stopped when the Soviet Union disintegrated and Kazakhstan gained its independence in 1991. Only then did the some 1.5 million people living in the area begin to realize the extent to which the testing affected the environment and their own health.

Lake Balkhash is another site of great environmental concern, for reasons similar to those affecting the Aral Sea. The largest lake in the eastern portion of Kazakhstan, Balkhash is a shallow body of water that has been seriously affected by agricultural projects and industrial production. Much of the problem stems from the misuse of the Ili River, which is the largest stream flowing into Lake Balkhash. Before it reaches Kazakhstan, the Ili's water is used for irrigation in China, where it is also exposed to contamination. Once in Kazakhstan, the Ili is additionally exposed to industrial pollution. Thus, to restore the quality of the river environment, both Kazakhstan's and China's governments must work together.

Kazakhstan's geography faces many environmental challenges, but, despite these problems and others, including geopolitical isolation, lack of access to the sea, and persistent (and increasing) aridity and desertification, Kazakhstan has the area and abundant resource base needed to develop a sound economy.

The Scythian tribe was one of the first peoples known to have lived in what is now Kazakhstan. Often described as a warlike group, the Scythians left records in the form of pictographs carved into stone, such as this one.

3

Kazakhstan Through Time

K azakhstan's history is interesting, yet, compared with some other parts of the world, not particularly complex. One might imagine that because of its size, the country must have a long and complicated past. However, the emergence of a Kazakh national identity occurred quite recently on the historical timeline.

Historical literature often mentions countries that were built at the crossroads of civilizations or important trade routes. These countries are usually smaller in size, perhaps because so many others wanted to acquire a piece of them. For centuries, it seemed that no one really cared much about the land of the Kazakh people. For thousands of years, tribes that eventually became the contemporary Kazakhs wandered through the steppes of Central Asia. This vast area, inhabited by small nomadic bands that had little of value to offer, were of no interest to the great conquerors. Other Central Asian locations, such as Bukhara and Samarkand, had much more to offer than did the pastoral nomadic tribes of Kazakhstan.

In the sixteenth century, tsarist Russia (then ruled by a tsar, equivalent to a British king or a dictator) forced its way east toward Kazakhstan. Eventually, all Kazak lands fell under Russian domination. Then, in the twentieth century, members of the Communist Party in Russia, who opposed the rule of the tsar, staged a revolution that eliminated the ruling house of Romanov and established what was to be 70 years of Soviet Communist domination of Kazakhstan.

The era of Soviet control brought many changes for the free-spirited, wandering Kazakhs. Ultimately, however, the Kazakhs were able to once again gain their freedom and this time they were able to establish a homeland free of foreign control. This chapter traces Kazakhstan's development over time, both from an historical as well as cultural standpoint.

A NOTE ON GEOPOLITICS

Before beginning a study of Kazakhstan's history, it is important to understand the nature of and relationship between culture, nationality, and political boundaries. Today many countries around the world share a common problem— their administrative borders (political boundaries) do not always follow the cultural (way of life) borders of all their residents. This results in groups of people who identify with a certain culture—a nationality, for example—living in areas, or countries, in which the predominant way of life is different. For example, most people living in the United States share the same culture as Anglo-Canadians living in Canada (Canadians originating from Great Britain rather than France), even though residents of the United States think of themselves as "Americans" and residents of Canada identify themselves as "Canadians." Problems arise, however, when people of differing cultures or nationalities live in a state that they do not govern.

This situation often results from colonialism or war. In

this case, both France and Britain colonized parts of what is now Canada. Ultimately, both English- and French-speaking people were united under one flag, in a Canada governed by the British colonists. French Canadians thus formed a minority population whose members even today often believe that they are not fairly treated. Many French Canadians strongly support secession, or withdrawing from Canada and forming an independent French-speaking country.

We tend to forget that Russia was no less an imperialistic force than were the British or French. The major difference was that Russia annexed its neighbors, whereas the United Kingdom and France developed colonies overseas. Soviet geopolitics also created new boundaries that repeatedly left large portions of particular ethnic groups outside of their original state (a politically-governed territory, including "country"). This cultural "overlapping" and exclusion should be kept in mind when examining the history of Kazakhstan and its relationships with its other Central Asian neighbors that formerly were part of Soviet Union.

EARLY HISTORY

Very little is known about the early history of the Kazakhs. Nomadic people of the steppes live a radically different lifestyle than the more sedentary (residing in one place) people of big cities. Nomads often can carry all of their material possessions on their backs and usually have not had any formal education. They do not record their history in books and they do not have libraries that store a record of their existence. Therefore, what is known about their culture and history comes from outsiders, people with whom they have been in contact.

When outsiders interpret the way of life of people of another culture, there is much room for misunderstanding and error. In ancient times, the greatest historian in many people's eyes was a Greek named Herodotus. Herodotus lived during the fifth century B.C. and traveled extensively, taking notes on different peoples and cultures. He also listened to tales told by others who had traveled to faraway places and seen people unlike the Greeks.

As did Persian travelers of the time, Herodotus wrote about tribes that lived in the steppes lying beyond the Black Sea and Caspian Sea. At the time, Scythians were the dominant tribe inhabiting the area of the lower Volga and what is today's Kazakhstan. They were the first recorded pastoral nomadic group known to control the territory of modern Kazakhstan by military force. Chronicles of Persian and early Georgian kingdoms often described the Scythians as being fierce warriors. These skilled fighters posed a constant danger to their southern neighbors.

INDO-EUROPEAN INHABITANTS

Both archeological evidence and historical documents show that the Scythians belonged to an Iranian group of Indo-European peoples. They originated in Iran and later expanded northward, moving toward the south Russian steppes in the region north of the Caucasus Mountains. Their rule lasted only until a stronger power pushed them westward, away from what is present-day Kazakhstan. Sometime around the third century B.C., Mongol-related groups overtook the region. One of them was the tribe of Alani, which later moved west toward the hills of the Caucasus Mountains. Thus, in ancient times, Kazakhstan served as the corridor for migrating peoples going both east and west.

When Chinese archeologists discovered a large number of mummies in western China (an area closely connected to Kazakhstan) that were of Indo-European descent, it was a big surprise. Nobody expected to find Caucasoid (the biological race of most native European peoples) mummies that far east in Asia. The surprise was even bigger when scientists realized how old the mummies were. By using reliable dating methods, they were able to show that the mummies were more than three thousand years old. The combined aridity and sands of the Takla Makan desert had preserved the human remains. This discovery suggests that Indo-European migrants from the west had passed through the Kazakhstan territory and had left marks of their presence in the region long before it was documented in written historical records.

EARLY TURKISH-MONGOLIAN KINGDOMS AND ARAB CONQUEST

For almost two thousand years, Indo-Europeans would not rule over Kazakhstan, however. Between the end of the Scythians' dominance in the third century B.C. and the beginning of Russian expansion in the sixteenth century, various Turkic-Mongolian kingdoms held rule over Central Asia. From the mountains of Altai, on the border between Kazakhstan and Mongolia, they used force to triumph over local tribes and push them further west. Later, during the fourth century A.D., Huns (another Central Asian nomadic group) rapidly expanded over much of western Asia. These fierce warriors swept westward as far as France and Germany.

Invasions from the east continued during later centuries. Another group from the Altai region, the Turks, achieved control over Kazakhstan and established kaganates (tribal structure ruled by a supreme ruler, or khan). Evidence suggests that these institutions were well structured and organized. But, in the middle of the eighth century, Arab forces appeared in the southern provinces of Central Asia. In a short period of time they gained control over Turkmenistan and Uzbekistan, all the way to the Syr Darya River. However, they were never able to conquer the rest of Central Asia. In the northern steppes, different Turkic kaganates continued to replace each other as major powers over the region.

FORMATION OF OASIS SETTLEMENTS

When the Karluk Turks became rulers of Kazakhstan in the eighth century, they started organizing permanent settlements. After thousands of years of a purely nomadic culture, cities now were rising in Kazakhstan oases. Even though Arabs controlled the southern area, they did not spread north of the Syr Darya until the tenth century, when the Karakhanids, another Turkic group, replaced the Karluks. By that time economic prosperity had drastically increased in the oasis settlements, as is evident from the size of these early cities, in which populations of thousands were concentrated.

The acceptance of Islam, the religion of the Arabs, further helped the development of Central Asia. It brought better cultural connections with the flourishing civilizations of the Arab-controlled world. The Islamic connection helped to develop what became major centers of trade and education at Bukhara and Samarkhand in present-day Uzbekistan. Located on the famous Silk Route, these cities benefited from trade with both China and the Western world. In the thirteenth century the famous European traveler, Marco Polo, visited the region and witnessed its richness.

POLITICAL CHANGES AND MONGOL DOMINATION

Between the eleventh and thirteenth centuries, Kazakh lands were divided among different Mongol- and Turkic-controlled areas. Not until 1218 would Kazakhstan's nomads see a single major power rule over all Kazakh lands. In that year warriors led by the Mongol Genghis Khan successfully invaded nearly all of Central Asia. These Mongol warriors quickly changed the geopolitical picture of the then-known world.

The ability of the "Mongol hordes" to invade and conquer became almost legendary. No force in the world at that time was able to stop Genghis Khan's skilled horsemen. In a very brief period of time, the Mongols established the largest kingdom that the world had ever seen. Their dominance spread eastward to the Pacific Ocean, westward into Central Europe, and southward to the Indian Ocean.

Everyone feared the Mongols, and with good reason. To a civilization that had just begun to transform itself from a nomadic lifestyle to one with cities and settlements, the Mongol invasion was devastating. When their destruction of the Central Asian society was accomplished, the Mongol hordes left this region. They went on to conquer Iran and southwest Asia, as well as lands and peoples in Eastern Europe. They tended to use Kazakhstan and surrounding areas as a mere stopover on the road to the west. However, there was good reason for their not staying. Central Asia offered few riches and lacked the wealth of what then was the rest of the known world. The Mongols did not consider the region to be of much importance.

With the Mongol assault, cultural and economic development in the oases stagnated. Economic activity (always an indicator of cultural development) decreased and political institutions lost their significance. All political organizations came under the control of new rulers who did not bother to improve the living conditions of the local people—an approach used often throughout history by conquering peoples, including those during the era of European colonization.

The first person to recognize the military and political supremacy of nomadic peoples was the fourteenth-century Arab historian, Ibn Khaldun. Khaldun observed that nomadic peoples and their highly mobile and warlike culture almost always won when in conflict with the culture of sedentary oasis people. When nomads brought their lifestyle into urban areas, however, the result almost always was a decline in prosperity, order, and well-being.

Khaldun also noticed that within one generation, conquering nomads themselves would be absorbed by the urban way of life. Born into a sedentary culture, children of nomads had a different outlook than that of their ancestors. In the case of Kazakhstan and the rest of Central Asia, Ibn Khaldun certainly was right. It took Kazakhstan's oasis tribes a number of years to start rebuilding their culture after the Mongol conquest. Meanwhile, Genghis Khan died and left an enormous empire to his descendents to divide and rule as their own kingdoms. Once they settled down in a particular area, the Mongols began to slowly change. They often learned and accepted the culture of the local people, making their mark on the culture and social life of Kazakh tribes, while the tribes accepted some elements of everyday Mongol life. With peace, the oasis settlements once again began to develop economically.

The western kingdom, of which Kazakhstan became a part during the thirteenth century, came under control of Genghis Khan's grandson, Batu Khan. His kingdom was spread between the Siberian plains on the east and Poland on the west. The Central Asian provinces, called the lands of the Golden Horde, were also included in Batu Khan's empire. However, every time a huge empire exists, challenges often appear. One, called the White Horde, appeared in south-central Kazakhstan and coexisted with the Golden Horde (although paying tribute).

Toward the end of the fourteenth century, the two hordes became united for a short period of time. This unification of Central Asia with the rest of what once was Batu Khan's empire stimulated development in Kazakh lands. Around that time, what became the Kazakh national identity began to take form. In the oases, urban people once again began to organize their societies and develop their economies. At least a century would pass, however, before the Kazakhs would become a fully developed nationality or possess a strong sense of self-identity.

TIMUR'S CONQUESTS

Soon other invaders entered the region of Kazakhstan and made their influence felt. When Timur, or Tamerlane, the Turkic leader, and his forces conquered Central Asia in the last decade of the fourteenth century, the Golden and White Hordes ceased to exist. Timur created a large kingdom and established its capital in Samarkand. Today Samarkand is in eastern Uzbekistan, just south of Kazakhstan's border. Timur not only won over Mongolian kingdoms, but continued westward and ultimately defeated even the Ottoman Empire's sultan Bayazid in the battle of Ankara in 1402.

Circumstances in Central Asia after Timur's death in 1405 allowed the creation of several more hordes, this time led by Turkic tribes. One of them was Uzbek khanate, the first independent institution of local tribes in many years. The khanate's boundaries spread from the southern deserts of Kyzyl Kum and Muiun Kum northward to the southern Siberian taiga forest. Basically, it covered the central and eastern area of present-day Kazakhstan.

THE FIFTEENTH THROUGH SEVENTEENTH CENTURIES

During the 1430s, Abu'l Khayr (1428–1468) established himself as a leader of Uzbek khanate. During his reign, dynastic rule was the norm, as was fighting with outsiders. Finally, in the second part of the fifteenth century, Abu'l Khayr's grandson became strong enough to take control of the khanate. Tribal differences between the Kazakhs and Uzbeks, both of whom were living in the same region, caused antagonisms that continued through the end of the century. In their attempts to achieve control of cities on and near the Syr Darya, local strongmen kept the whole region in permanent turmoil.

Because of the ongoing political chaos in the region, it is impossible to determine a precise date for the formation of the Kazakh khanate. Historians generally agree that it happened sometime around the turn of the sixteenth century. Once it was formed, the Kazakh khanate was ready to spread its influence over its Central Asian neighbors. The most logical expansion was toward the south. There, they could continue the battle with Uzbek leaders for dominance over the Syr Darya and various trade routes.

As was mentioned previously, the early sixteenth century was the period during which the modern Kazakh identity began to form. The fact that inhabitants of the Kazakh khanate's area belonged to the same cultural group was in their favor. All of them used Turkic languages to communicate. Using a "neutral" language was essential during the early stages

The mausoleum of Khoja Akhmed Yasavi in Turkestan, Kazakhstan, is considered sacred by the people of the nation. Used as the capital of the Kazakh khanate from the sixteenth to the eighteenth century, Turkestan holds a special place in Kazakhstan's history.

of expansion, and doing so helped to further spread the khanate's influence and political control.

Since Kazakhs belonged to one territorial unit, they were able to recognize themselves as one nation, or one homogenous group of people. They were able to distinguish their own ethnicity (culture and sense of self-identity) from that of their neighbors, most importantly the Uzbeks. In this context, it is important to understand the nature of the Kazakh khanate. It was not a political unit with rigid boundaries but rather a union of tribal groups with different ancestry (although sharing a common language) occupying a geographical area with vague and ever-changing boundaries.

THE LAST KAZAKH KHANATE

The Kazakh khanate would form federation-type organizations with a primary goal of providing military protection for tribes and clans. At the same time, on the historical time-scale, Europe was experiencing the early beginnings of nation-states. Such states were a product of the political unification of a single ethnic group or nation. In a nation-state, the nation (a territory occupied by a nationality of peoples) becomes a self-governed political unit (state) as well. In the Kazakh steppes, however, people were divided into tribes and clans that often were not closely related to each other. Under these circumstances, political changes often happened quickly. The many changes in political dominance, territorial control, and ethnic conflict present a nightmare for modern historians who attempt to unravel the region's very complex history.

During the sixteenth century, Kazakhs divided into three hordes: the Greater, Middle, and Lesser. This process of political transformation was based simply on geographical circumstances. Historians agree that because of the vast size of the territory they occupied, Kazakhs divided the land into different political units. Although divided administratively, however, they continued to preserve the same cultural characteristics and sense of unity. This unity lasted until the eighteenth century and the first encounters with the Russians.

Even though Kazakh independence lasted only until the beginning of the eighteenth century, the people of Kazakhstan were able in the process to build a strong sense of ethnic identity.

RUSSIAN INTERVENTION

When the Kalmyks invaded and occupied some Kazakh lands in the second part of the seventeenth century, it became obvious that the khanate would not survive. Until the 1730s, the Kalmyks were in position to control all of Kazakhstan. Finally, searching for protection from the Kalmyks, the Kazakhs asked the Russian tsar (czar) for help. This act marked the beginning of Russian imperialism in Central Asia. The tsar used the opportunity to expand Russia's influence toward the Kazakh steppes by sending military help and later annexing the territory.

During the next two centuries, Russian military expeditions built a number of fortresses in south Siberia and north Kazakhstan (which later became important towns). Semipalatinsk, Omsk, and Ursk-Kamenogorsk were all built over a three-year period in the 1700s. Kazakhs became increasingly dependent upon the Russian military presence. Beginning with its annexation of the Small Horde during the eighteenth century, Russia slowly but successfully spread its control over Kazakhstan.

Many Russian settlers (most of whom came with the military) began to realize the agricultural potential that Kazakh land offered. During the reign of Catherine II, many Russian Cossacks were sent to the frontier. There, they protected the interests of the Russian Empire and helped continue its eastward spread.

Kazakhs and Cossacks should not be considered the same group of people. Kazakhs, as has been discussed, emerged as an ethnic group of Asian stock. Cossacks, on the other hand, served as a military order of European origin. They were ethnic Slavs who practiced Orthodox Christianity. Cossacks still exist in Russia today, although their significance is not as great as it once was. During tsarist times, Cossacks were usually given land and other privileges in exchange for military service. They were, as they proudly said, responsible to nobody but the Russian tsars.

NINETEENTH-CENTURY KAZAKHSTAN

In the nineteenth century, Russian colonization increased and peasants from European areas increasingly started moving toward newly controlled Asian territories. The steady stream of European Russian peasants moving eastward in search of lands continued into the twentieth century. During the 1860s, the government established new administrative divisions that divided Kazakhstan in several regions. European colonizers

The Kazakh people were originally part of an Asian ethnic population. The style of dress seen in this picture of eighteenth-century public figure Tole Bi shows hints of that Asian heritage.

used this opportunity to claim and occupy the best agricultural land in the northern portions of Kazakhstan.

Today's demographic picture of the rural areas in Kazakhstan's north and northwest still reflects the impact of Russian colonization. By the end of the nineteenth century, Kazakhstan had over 500 settlements populated mainly by Europeans. Kazakhs, most of whom still practiced a pastoral nomadic lifestyle, did not consider settled farming to be an alternative to their existing way of life. Yet they were rapidly losing their pastureland to the Russian farmers. Since independent Kazakh political institutions did not exist outside of Russian supervision, there was nothing that could stop this process. In addition to this already alarming situation, the nomads received another near fatal blow. A Russian land grab, called Stolypin's Agrarian Reform (1906–1912), reserved over 40 million acres of Kazakhstan's land for agriculture.

FROM RUSSIAN EMPIRE TO SOVIET UNION

The early twentieth century provided further challenges to the Kazakh dream of independence. Kazakhstan's political establishment at the time enjoyed many benefits from its connections with the Russian aristocracy. At the same time, the position of ordinary people worsened. When World War I struck in the early 1900s, and the Russian tsarist government decided to draft young Kazakhs into military service, riots erupted. Until 1916, Kazakhs had been excluded from military service in the Russian army. But, because of Russia's losses in the war with Germany, the country desperately needed to draft more soldiers. When the Russians turned to the Kazakhs for troops, tens of thousands of people participated in the resistance against Russian military garrisons.

Led by the Alash Orda political party, Kazakhs attempted to take advantage of what appeared to be a golden opportunity. Russia was deeply immersed in its own internal political turmoil. In February 1917, political chaos in Russia erupted into a full-scale revolution. The Kazakhs hoped to use Russia's internal disarray to gain their own autonomy. As happened in other provinces of the Russian Empire, however, Kazakhstan's attempt to become independent was short-lived.

KAZAKHSTAN AS A SOVIET REPUBLIC

During its 1917 revolution, Russia was taken over by the rebel Bolsheviks (communists). By 1920, the Bolsheviks had gained control over the Kazakh region and incorporated it into a new country, the Soviet Union. Soon, the steppes would become the destination for other types of European settlers. When Kazakhstan became an autonomous Soviet territory (under the name of Kirghiz ASSR until 1925), the Soviets began sending various political prisoners there. They also sent people from a number of ethnic groups that were being displaced from their homes in the European regions of the USSR.

The final political transformation of Kazakhstan within the Soviet Union came in 1936, when the Soviet government created the Kazakh Soviet Socialist Republic, with borders matching today's Kazakhstan.

Later, during and after World War II, the Kazakhs further lost influence over their republic's affairs. Both political and economic decisions were made in distant Moscow, regardless of local concerns, by the Communist government. The Soviet regime continued to send hundreds of thousands of people to Kazakhstan for resettlement. Until the end of the Soviet Union's rule in 1991, Kazakhstan's political existence was very tightly tied to Moscow. During the 1980s, however, it became increasingly apparent that Kazakhstan would eventually gain greater autonomy, possibly even independence.

INDEPENDENCE

In 1986, Soviet leader Mikhail Gorbachev replaced a native Kazakh with a Russian as head of Kazakhstan's government. When this happened, rioters took to the streets of Almaty, Kazakhstan's capital city. The police finally regained control, but not until hundreds of people had lost their lives. Several years later, in 1990, the Union of Soviet Socialist Republics began to break up. In 1991, the Soviet Union dissolved as a political entity. In December 1991, Kazakhstan proclaimed its independence— the last of the former Soviet Republics to do so. With independence, voters elected a native Kazakh, Nursultan Nazarbayev, to lead them toward the twenty-first century.

Most of the games that are popular in Kazakhstan involve horseback riding.
The national game is called "Kyz-koo," or "Catch the Girl." Two Kazakh
people are seen playing the game during a celebration for the 1,500th
birthday of the city of Turkestan.

4

People and Culture

For most people in Kazakhstan, life did not change dramatically until their homeland became integrated into the Soviet Union. Throughout the previous centuries, generations of Kazakhs enjoyed the lifestyle of pastoral nomads surviving in the predominantly semiarid steppe grassland. Life here was much different than that among the sedentary groups living in neighboring Uzbekistan or Russia. The nomads' most important economic activity was livestock grazing and their most valuable property was their horse (and eagles for hunting).

EUROPEAN CULTURAL INFLUENCE

During the nineteenth century, the Russian military slowly, yet successfully, overtook not just the Kazakhstan steppes, but also all neighboring territories. It marked the beginning of European influence on Turkic-Mongolian Central Asian ethnic groups. The USSR's policy of internationalism brought major changes to the lives of the Kazakh peoples. The development of numerous towns and industries, together with the rapid spread of crop agriculture, rapidly ate away at the open grasslands. The number of nomads was drastically reduced, and the number of urban Kazakhs increased. However, after 70 years of communism and more than a decade of postcommunism, Kazakhstan (and perhaps Mongolia) remains the only country in the world with a substantial number of nomads who still live lives identical to those of their ancestors centuries ago.

PEOPLES OF KAZAKHSTAN

Before the breakup of the Soviet Union, Kazakhstan was the USSR's leading multiethnic republic. In the USSR, republics were formed based on ethnicity. A dominant ethnic group—usually the one for which the republic was named—had to have a population majority of more than 50 percent. Kazakhstan was unique in that it was the only autonomous republic within the USSR in which the ethnic group for which it was named did not hold a majority of 50 percent or more. In 1989, ethnic Kazakhs accounted for only some 40 percent of Kazakhstan's 17 million inhabitants. Although peoples of European stock were in the minority in pre–World War II Kazakhstan, they managed to account for over 50 percent of the population in 1989. Today, however, the Kazakh population has increased its proportion to about 53 percent of the country's population, which now stands at approximately 15 million. Much of this gain is the result of ethnic Russians leaving Kazakhstan after the country gained its independence. Kazakhstan has always been a country in which migration, not birthrate, was the primary factor influencing population change.

Many of the ethnic groups that were not native to the republic had been deported from European Russia (in the Soviet Union) as a result of Joseph Stalin's anti-Nazi decrees. Millions of

Volga Germans, Crimean Tatars, Chechens, and other enemies of the Soviet Revolution were sent to Kazakhstan because of their supposed collaboration, real or potential, with the German occupation force. In addition, during the 1950s and 1960s, the Soviets promoted a Virgin Lands project in which new areas were opened to grain farming. Thousands of people were sent to Kazakhstan to develop the country's second "breadbasket" (the first was in Ukraine). When the Soviet Union disintegrated, however, Kazakhstan developed its own immigration policy.

In Kazakhstan, dual citizenship (Russian and Kazakh) quickly became an issue of heated political discussion. The government of Kazakhstan decided not to grant Russians the dual citizenship option. Residents had to choose whether they wanted to be citizens of Kazakhstan or of Russia. This policy, and the lack of economic opportunity, triggered a massive emigration (departure) of Kazakhstan's Russians. The country's ethnic Russian population decreased by more than 25 percent between 1989 and 1999. During the same period, the ethnic Kazakh population increased by almost 23 percent. A substantial number of ethnic Kazakhs immigrated into the country from other former republics and Mongolia.

One minority ethnic group that achieved a significant increase in population was the Uzbeks. Their success in Kazakhstan's business life and their ability to speak the local language were important factors that helped stimulate immigration. The ethnic group that lost two-thirds of its pre-1991 Kazakhstan population was the Germans, many of whom returned to their homeland after the reunification of the former East and West Germany.

POPULATION DENSITY

With a population density of only 14 persons per square mile, Kazakhstan is a very sparsely populated country. By comparison, the United States has a population density of 78 persons per square mile, and the world's average is about 180 persons per square mile. Although its rate of natural population increase (births) shows an annual increase, Kazakhstan is actually losing population because of heavy emigration (out-migration). The growth rate is sharply divided along ethnic lines. Russian and Ukrainian couples have many fewer children, on average, than do Kazakhs.

Compared with the rest of the central and southern Asian countries, birthrates in Kazakhstan are the lowest in the region. This condition no doubt results from the fact that urban families tend to have much smaller families than do rural people. In the region considered, only Iran has a higher percentage of its population classified as urban (64 percent versus Kazakhstan's 56 percent).

Life expectancy at birth in Kazakhstan is 66 years—60 for males and 71 for females. The span of 11 years between male and female life expectancy is one of the greatest in the world.

NATIONALITY	POPULATION (MILLIONS)		POPULATION CHANGE		PERCENTAGE OF TOTAL POPULATION	
	1989	1999	(MILLIONS)	(%)	1989	1999
Kazakh	6.496	7.985	1.488	22.9	40.1	53.4
Russian	6.062	4.479	−1.582	−26.1	37.4	30.0
Ukrainian	0.875	0.547	−0.328	−37.5	5.4	3.7
Uzbek	0.331	0.370	39.6	12.0	2.0	2.5
German	0.946	0.353	−0.593	−62.7	5.8	2.4
Tatar	0.320	0.249	0.071	−22.4	2.0	1.7
Uighur	0.181	0.210	28.8	15.9	1.1	1.4

Source: *Agency of the Republic of Kazakhstan on Statistic.*
http://www.kazstat.asdc.kz/.

Note: Only nationalities that represent over 1% of the total population are included in the table. However, over 40 different nationalities accounted for in the census live in Kazakhstan today.

Figure 1: Population of Kazakhstan by Nationality, 1989 and 1999

Demographers (scientists who study the human population) have a number of theories attempting to explain the huge gap, but no one really knows why Kazakh women, on average, live 11 years longer then men.

LANGUAGE

Since at least the sixth century, people living in Kazakhstan used different forms of the Turkic language to communicate. However, because in nomadic life written documents are very rare, it has been impossible for linguists (people who study language) to track down the earliest beginning of Turkic languages. Even though Kazakhs descend from people of Mongolian stock, they accepted Turkic as their tongue. During the Arabic expansion to Central Asia during the eighth and ninth centuries A.D., Arabic became the language of intellectuals and literature. But Arabic did not permanently spread to the nomads of the Kazakh steppes. It was, however, adopted by many sedentary farming people living in oases.

Finally, during the second half of the nineteenth century, the Russian language was spread throughout much of Central Asia, and at the turn of the twentieth century Kazakh was one of only three Central Asian languages with a literary form. Created in the middle of the nineteenth century, Kazakh was used by writers Abay Kunanbay (1845–1904) and Chokan Valikhan (1837–1865).

Even so, among the Soviet republics of the USSR, Russian became the *lingua franca* (single language used to communicate among peoples speaking many different tongues). It was widely used in Kazakhstan, especially because for some time the majority of citizens in the republic spoke Russian as their native tongue.

After independence, the Kazakhstan government placed emphasis on making Kazakh the official language. Although Russian continues to be the dominant language of business, it is losing its influence in Kazakhstan. Very few ethnic Russians are fluent in Kazakh, and most show no interest in learning the language. Thus, the government policy encouraging the use of Kazakh serves as an additional reason for Russians to leave the country.

The official script in Kazakhstan is still the Russian Cyrillic alphabet with several Kazakh symbols added.

RELIGION

For a country with so many different nationalities among its population, it is not surprising that Kazakhstan's peoples practice a number of different religions. Among the various faiths, Islam and Christianity dominate in Central Asia. Islam, introduced a millennium earlier than Christianity in the region, has been the dominant religion among sedentary oases and urban dwellers since the eighth century. Arab expansion spread Islam quickly throughout the region, where local rulers accepted the faith in order to gain personal benefits. Most trade routes and the most important political connections were under the control of Islamic people. The influence of Islam spread from Samarkand and Bukhara northward into the steppes. Long before the Russians entered Kazakhstan, nearly all Kazakhs were nominally Muslim.

The rapid spread of Islam among the Kazakhs may have been spurred by an interesting fact of cultural history. Many Kazakhs had previously worshipped a monotheistic (one god) deity named Taingir. Therefore, the idea of a single god, also predominant in Islam, was not new to them. There are, however, major differences between the Islamic religious practices of Central Asians, particularly Kazakhs, and Southwest Asians, where Islam originated.

During 70 years of life as part of the Soviet Union—an officially atheist state—several generations of Kazakhs were not encouraged to practice the religions of their ancestors. After independence, President Nursultan Nazarbayev pro-claimed Kazakhstan to be a secular (not religious) state. His

Most of the people of Kazakhstan are Muslims, although their faith differs in certain aspects from the type of Islam practiced in many other countries. Although the nation is secular, religion is taken very seriously. The opening of a new mosque like this one is cause for a large celebration.

goal was to preserve tight political control and eliminate any opposition, since in predominantly Muslim countries, opposition often grows within religious circles. Since the early 1990s, however, dozens of new mosques have been built throughout Kazakhstan. Many have been gifts from Saudi Arabia, Egypt, and other countries that actively support an Islamic renaissance in Central Asia. President Nazarbayev allowed these types of gifts because of the financial stimulus they provided.

However, since many of Kazakhstan's pastoral nomads still organize their beliefs around the ancient animistic worship of different spirits, many of the donated mosques are often half empty, something rarely seen elsewhere in the Islamic world.

Religious orientation is closely tied to ethnicity. The majority of Slavs in Kazakhstan belong to the Eastern Orthodox Church, and it is rare to see an ethnic Russian or Ukrainian practicing Islam. Christianity, as did Islam, arrived in Central Asia with military expeditions. Initially, its practice was limited to towns with a Russian military presence. Later, when farmers from European provinces came to Kazakhstan, they brought their religious practices. This religious diffusion from Eastern Europe continued with the industrial development of Kazakhstan and the immigration of other peoples during the twentieth century.

Today, Russian and Ukrainian Orthodox churches are present in many towns. So, too, are Protestant and Roman Catholic churches that were built by Germans and Koreans. Much to its credit, after independence Kazakhstan was able to preserve religious tolerance among so many different groups without major excesses and ethnic confrontations. In some other parts of the former Soviet Union, religion-driven conflicts are common. In Kazakhstan, however, people resisted the temptation to erode religious harmony.

One factor that may help to explain the Kazakhs' generally passive attitude toward religion is the organization of its dominant social structure. The life of the individual centers primarily around family, clan, and tribe. Religion plays a lesser role. This is especially true of the nomadic Kazakhs, although it also is true among many sedentary urban dwellers.

LIFE IN THE STEPPES

As already discussed, until the twentieth century, most Kazakhs were pastoral nomads who wandered the vast steppe grasslands that spread some 1,400 miles (2,250 kilometers) across Kazakhstan. Life can be very difficult in the steppes. The climate is harsh and there is a constant need to improvise and adapt in order to survive. Each year, in the early spring and then again during the fall, tribes and clans migrate hundreds of miles in search of the best grazing land for their livestock. Some groups, it is recorded, have migrated more than 1,000 miles (1,610 kilometers) during a single year. On the 470 million acres (195 million hectares) of land still available for grazing, nomads herd a variety of animals, including horses, sheep, camels, goat, cattle, and yaks.

Among the Kazakh nomads, a herder's economic status is based on how many head of livestock are in his possession. Although sheep provide much of the food for nomadic tribes, horses are especially prized. Local horse breeds are highly durable, and good horses are essential to the nomadic way of life. Their importance is symbolized in many stories and songs handed down from generation to generation.

During their constant migration, Kazakhs carry all of their material possessions, including their dwellings, called yurts, which are rebuilt each time they establish a camp. A yurt is a tentlike structure, but one that is much more complex than the ordinary tent. The dwelling's origin is not known. Some scholars believe that they were first used as early as the sixth century B.C. During the long, cold winter months, family members spend their time in the yurt working and preparing for spring. Since yurts are an essential part of nomads' lives, their role has a spiritual character. The way yurts are built, including the arrangement of all of its parts,

Kazakh nomads live in traditional structures called yurts, like the one seen in this photograph. The yurt is similar to a tent, but is much sturdier and has a more complex interior.

strictly follows deeply established symbolism and traditional tribal beliefs.

Kazakh nomads show high respect for their elders and guests. In this patriarchal traditional society, life in the yurts is organized hierarchically. Each person, including highly respected guests, must know where his or her seat is.

Hospitality is of tremendous importance in the Kazakh society. Guests, expected or not, are always welcomed. On such occasions, the host usually sets the *dastraqan*, a table full of different dishes. This custom is common to many traditional cultures, although in different forms.

Hosts always bring their best food for the guests. The diet of nomads has changed little over the centuries, while in the urban areas, diets have changed somewhat as Western and other products have found their way to grocery stores. Nomadic Kazakh food is basically quite simple. It lacks the complexity of many of the more exotic cuisines such as French or Italian, but its main dishes are bold yet both nutritious and delicious. They include different versions of meat products, salads, marinated vegetables, and fried or baked bread.

Milk products are also important in the steppes because of their availability. Milk itself is consumed in a variety of ways: it is drunk straight, or as the chief ingredient of various prepared drinks. Cheese and yogurt also are a regular part of the diet. A very popular drink, called koumiss (kumys), is made of fermented milk. This is an alcoholic drink that is very popular among inhabitants of the Kazakh steppes. Tea is also an important part of the Kazakhs' diet. Depending on local customs and availability, sugar or milk may be added to the tea, which is served in bowls. Vodka is very popular with Kazakhstan's Russian population and is becoming a widely consumed alcoholic drink particularly among urban Kazakhs.

Not much free time is available to the nomadic people of Kazakhstan. Hard living conditions usually keep them busy, but when it is time for leisure, it is a group activity. One of the most popular sports is wrestling, several versions of which can be found in Kazakhstan. Perhaps because of the importance of horses in their society, Kazakhs love to wrestle while on horseback. To stay in the saddle and win requires tremendous balance and skill. Most of the popular activities involve skilled horseback riding. In one game, riders must pick up a small bag from the ground while riding at full gallop. In another, riders play a polo-like game with the body of a goat by trying to gain possession of it.

Outside of the steppes, people enjoy various summer and winter sports, from skiing and skating to hiking in the mountains.

A popular and somewhat dangerous Kazakh sport is Tenge-alu. In this ancient competitive game, a player rides a horse at a full gallop and attempts to pick up some money that lies on the ground. The money is the player's prize.

Hunting, for both big and small game, is enjoyed all over the country. Kazakhs, who are experts in hunting, have developed *berkutchi*, which is fox hunting with eagles or hawks. After they are caught as young birds, eagles are trained by their masters to hunt foxes, or different types of birds. Eagle hunting requires well-developed skills on the part of the hunter that are passed down from generation to generation within families.

ARTS AND ARCHITECTURE

Since the Kazakh language did not have a written form until the nineteenth century, most of the cultural history was preserved and passed down from generation to generation in oral form. Traveling singers and storytellers called *akyns* used music to tell about past times, heroic war stories, or love stories. They would visit settlements accompanied with other performers and entertain the public. On holidays and at festivals, *akyns* organized poetry competitions. They would compete with one another in an event called *aytis*, which is one of the Kazakhs' most popular folklore events. The importance of *akyns* to the Kazakh tradition is evidenced by the fact that the country's national holiday is the birthday of one its greatest poets, Zhambyl Zhabayev.

Kazakh music employs more than 50 native instruments. One of them, the bowed-string *kobyz,* is considered to be an ancestor of European string instruments. It is believed that the kobyz is one of the oldest instruments in the world still in widespread use. Developed by shamans in ancient times, the *kobyz* is still one of the most popular instruments in Kazakhstan.

In the twentieth century, especially during the Soviet era, Kazakhstan experienced a tremendous increase in the development of music, ballet, opera, and theater. Today, the country hosts many different international events. Some spotlight Kazakh culture, but many others focus on traditions introduced by Russians, Germans, Koreans, Uighurs, and others.

Throughout most of Kazakhstan's history, its architecture, such as the yurt, was traditional. In urban centers, stylish departures from traditional forms were limited to sacred sites, such as churches or mosques. This changed in the twentieth century, especially during the period of rapid urban expansion introduced by the Soviets. A distinctive architecture, called the Socialist realism style, produced chainlike units of bold, gray, concrete buildings of monumental size. During the past few years, however, different designs have appeared in Almaty and in Astana, where the government is building the newly established capital.

LITERATURE

Most of Kazakhstan's early literary works were written in Arabic in mosques and religious schools. Writing in the Kazakh language did not begin until the second half of the nineteenth century. The development of a domestic Kazakh literature, therefore, is quite recent, a tradition less than 150 years old. The great Kazakh poet Abay Kunanbayev (1845–1904) is commonly called the "father of Kazakh literature." He played a leading role in establishing the Kazakh literary tradition. Many people regard Kunanbayev as the most famous Kazakh in history.

Kunanbayev was one of the first members of Kazakhstan's secular elite. He was a well-educated composer and educator as well as a poet. Some of his poems were critical of the traditional Kazakh way of life. Kunanbayev also greatly admired Russian culture. He strongly supported a close friendship between the Russians and his own people. His writings helped pave the way for the Soviet-imposed economic, social, and political changes of the twentieth century. Kunanbayev's ideas were best expressed in his collection of essays called *Edifications*. After his death, another great playwright, author, and novelist, Mukhtar Auezov (1897–1961), followed Kunanbayev's path, becoming a leading figure of Kazakhstan's Soviet-era literature. However, during the period of Stalin's leadership in the Soviet Union, many representatives of the Kazakh vanguard, led by Akhmet Baytursunov, were sent to prison because of their writings.

EDUCATION

Despite its many shortcomings, Soviet communism did have a least one positive aspect: it recognized the importance of formal education. During the Soviet era, many educational institutions were developed and great emphasis was placed on each individual becoming educated. Before the formation of the Soviet Union, Kazakhstan's dominantly nomadic population had little opportunity or need for formal education. Today there are many fine elementary and secondary schools, and several large universities. The country boasts more than 11,000 public libraries housing millions of documents.

Primary and secondary education is free and most children are enrolled. Private education, although conducted under government supervision, is available and the number of students in private schools is growing. The Al-Farabi State University in Almaty is the largest institution of higher learning in the country. It is one of two major universities in Kazakhstan; the other is Karaganda.

In this 1999 photograph, a Kazakh woman sells newspapers as she stands below an election poster that supported Dukesh Baimbetov, then a candidate for the parliament of Kazakhstan.

CHAPTER

5

Government

lthough it was the last of the former Soviet Union's republics to proclaim independence, Kazakhstan did not waste time in adopting a democratic government. The first democratically held presidential elections established an ethnic Kazakh as the country's president. Such an event was considered a huge success for the Kazakhs, who, at that time, were an ethnic minority in their own country. During the Soviet era, Slavic Russians, Ukrainians, and White Russians composed the ethnic majority.

At that time, in the early 1990s, the perception of Kazakhstan in the West was very positive. Even though it was the only Muslim-dominated country among the newly independent former Soviet republics that possessed nuclear weapons, Kazakhstan chose a pacifist policy. The size of its army was reduced, ethnic tensions were minimal, and Western companies were invited to invest in energy production industries. Democracy seemed to be developing at a proper pace. Yet, as has happened in most other former Soviet republics, the postcommunist-era opportunities have not adequately been fulfilled. Today, Kazakhstan still lags far behind the world's developed countries. Much of the problem has to do with inept government and widespread corruption.

BRANCHES OF GOVERNMENT

The distribution of political power in Kazakhstan is similar to that in the United States. There are three branches of government: executive, legislative, and judicial. Each branch has equal freedom to act in the political process. The legislative branch is represented by Kazakhstan's equivalent of the U.S. Congress. It creates new laws approved by vote of its members. The executive branch includes the president of the country, a prime minister, and members of the council of ministers, whose function is to implement new laws and to "take care of every day's business." The Supreme Court is representative of the judicial branch. It controls, regulates, and mediates important decisions.

Young democracies attempting to develop in postcommunist societies tend to be quite different than the older, well-established democracies of Western nations. Sometimes a huge gap divides democratic ideals and actual political reality. Often, the executive branch of government is at fault. Corruption is rampant. Nepotism, the hiring of family members, is a common practice. And country leaders are often authoritarian, exercising much more power than they are granted by the constitution. The executive branch often blocks the work of other governmental units, while at the same time accumulating power—and often wealth—in its own hands. Many of the Central Asian countries, including Kazakhstan, have followed this path. Even though they all became somewhat democratic in the early 1990s, they all have fallen into this trap.

Today, the presidents of neighboring Uzbekistan and Turkmenistan are becoming increasingly despotic. They hold great power and have created a legal form of dictatorship simply by having the legislature pass a law establishing a "president for life" position. In this context, it must be mentioned that all presidents of Central Asian countries came from the old Communist apparatus of the Soviet era. Once they were elected to office, they did not consider the eventual surrender of power by democratic methods.

THE PRESIDENT

The president of Kazakhstan at this writing—and the only one elected to this office since the country's independence in 1991—is Nursultan Nazarbayev. A product of the earlier Communist political system, Nazarbayev has been active in politics since the late 1970s. A highly skilled politician, he was able to climb the Communist Party ladder to its highest position in Kazakhstan. With independence, Nazarbayev used his experience and recognition to attract enough votes to be elected president. Soon he engineered a number of constitutional changes that resulted in the loss of many elements of traditional democracy. After changes to the constitution in 1993 and 1995, president Nazarbayev's power was drastically expanded and that of the legislative branch (parliament) was significantly reduced.

The president is both the head of state and commander of the armed forces. He also has the power to block any of the parliament's legislation. The office of prime minister is secondary to that of president. Although the holder of this office is nominally the head of government, the president holds the power and can override any decisions made by the prime minister. In 1999, Nazarbayev was reelected to a seven-year term as president, receiving 81 percent of the vote. Many foreign observers, however, called the election "well below acceptable international standards."

Nursultan Nazarbayev is the current president of Kazakhstan. Seen here at his January 1999 inauguration, Nazarbayev followed the ancient Kazakh custom of standing on a piece of white felt material that symbolizes the pure and uncorrupted thoughts of the newly chosen leader.

In 2001, Nazarbayev's son-in-law, Rakhat Aliev, was accused of financial misconduct in a governmental position, but he was never prosecuted. Instead, he was transferred to another position and workplace. Because of obvious corruption at the highest level, Kazakhstan's political and economical development has suffered greatly. The great hope for the country held by so many people a decade earlier simply has not been fulfilled. Not only does President Nazarbayev maintain a tight grip on the country's government, but his family members control many important industries, including banking, the oil industry, and the media.

PARLIAMENT AND THE ADMINISTRATIVE BRANCH

Kazakhstan is a presidential, rather than parliamentary, democracy. This means that the parliament has minimal power. It is a bicameral (two branches) parliament, with the *Mazhilis*, or lower house, and Senate. Members of the Mazhilis are elected by popular vote from the districts they represent. Members of the Senate are elected from the 16 administrative divisions. Moreover, the president holds the right to appoint seven additional senators.

Kazakhstan is divided into 14 oblasts (the equivalent of states in the United States) and the two city districts of Almaty and Astana. The president appoints the governors of the provinces and oblasts. The chief executive of the oblasts in which Almaty and Astana are located appoints chief executives for these cities. For decades, Kazakhstan's capital was in Almaty, its largest city, located in the far southeastern corner of the country. In 1998, however, the government decided to move the capital to Astana, a more centrally located city.

THE JUDICIAL BRANCH

In 1995 Kazakhstan's constitution was changed to divide the country's judicial branch into two courts: the Supreme Court and the Constitutional Council. In theory, at least, the Supreme Court's responsibilities are very similar to those of the U.S. Supreme Court. It holds the final word in interpreting the country's laws. The Constitutional Council rules over irregularities in the political process. The country's president appoints the chairman of the Council, who is the most powerful judge of the seven in the group.

The Constitutional Council's main responsibility is to

make decisions in cases of election fraud and other unconstitutional activities by any political party or individual. The president, of course, can strongly influence, if not control, this body's membership through appointments and other means. The body's credibility was further eroded in 1995 when the constitution was changed to give all former presidents a seat on the Council.

FOREIGN POLICY AND THE ARMED FORCES

During the existence of the Soviet Union, Kazakhstan was a strategically important region. The republic used to accommodate a huge number of Red Army soldiers, whose main activity was to patrol the always sensitive border region with China. Also, many other military-related activities were based in Kazakhstan. Two of the best known were the airspace center in Baikonur, and the nuclear laboratory and testing center in Semipalatinsk. Finally, nuclear warheads were installed throughout the republic's territory during the Cold War.

After independence, Kazakhstan used the opportunity to reduce the size of its army and navy. The country concentrated on the development of peaceful relationships with its neighbors, especially Russia, China, and Uzbekistan, and military training is still organized in cooperation with the Russian army. In June 2002, Kazakhstan held a multinational conference at which, among other things, the major issue was the prevention of a potential war between Pakistan and India.

The country is very active in the field of foreign policy. It was able to establish itself as a member of various organizations, including the United Nations, Commonwealth of Independent States, Organization on Security and Cooperation in Europe, and Partnership for Peace (NATO). The United States was the first country in the world to formally recognize the Kazakhstan's independent existence within the international community of nations. The U.S. embassy was opened only three months after Kazakhstan declared its independence in December 1991. Relationships between the United States and Kazakhstan remain good. Mutual interests and concerns include joint work on security issues, the reduction of nuclear weapons, and trade, particularly that involving the growing energy sector of the Kazakh economy.

A huge part of Kazakhstan's economy depends on oil and natural gas reserves in the Caspian Sea region. Seen here is Tengiz, Kazakhstan's largest oil field. The rectangular slabs are made of hardened sulfur, a by-product of a poisonous gas that is found with the oil pumped at the field.

6

Economy

I n the early 1990s, the economies of the newly independent former socialist republics of the Soviet Union experienced a sharp downturn. The transformation from a centrally (government) planned economy toward free enterprise (market-driven economy) appeared to be a painful process. What had been a huge Soviet domestic market with almost 300 million consumers suddenly became tremendously smaller, depending on the size of the republic. Additionally, many of the new countries experienced some form of ethnic conflict. This, too, hindered the stability that is essential to economic development. In Kazakhstan, however, these problems presented no real handicap to economic growth. The country's large size, population, industrial potential, and few ethnic antagonisms all worked to its advantage.

Western economic experts openly supported Kazakhstan's

development and foreign investments. Everybody expected that the country would experience a remarkable economic transformation. Sadly, however, the country's economic potential has not been realized. Poor government and uncontrolled corruption at all levels have taken a severe toll. (Similar problems exist in nearly all of the former Soviet republics.)

Kazakhstan still has a very long way to go if it is to become a developed country. The country is highly dependent upon energy production, and its oil and natural gas production account for nearly one-third of the country's annual revenue. This dependence makes the economy highly vulnerable: dependence on a single resource such as oil can cause a huge financial shock if prices suddenly drop. Fortunately, however, because of high oil prices on the world market, the economy reached a peak in 2000 and 2001.

For the time being, the Kazakh government appears to have used its oil profits wisely. For example, it was able to pay off its $400 million loan from the International Monetary Fund seven years ahead of time. No other former Soviet republic can match this level of financial responsibility.

ENERGY

Ever since oil resources were discovered in Baku, Azerbaijan, at the turn of the twentieth century, it was obvious that the Caspian basin held huge reserves. During the 70-year history of the Soviet Union, no one outside of the country was informed of exactly how much. The Soviet government did not allow any foreigners to invest in petroleum research, exploration, or development. This policy changed in the early 1990s, with the breakup of the USSR. It soon became apparent that the Caspian region held some of the world's richest oil and natural gas reserves. In the northeastern portion of the Caspian Sea, which belongs to Kazakhstan, giant oil fields were discovered.

Kazakhstan also produces a significant amount of coal

that provides an additional source of export revenue. During Soviet times, only Russia and the Ukraine were producing more coal than Kazakhstan. Enough electrical energy is produced by various means to meet domestic demands. However, the country's energy sector suffers somewhat from an obvious lack of infrastructure. Its distribution network is poorly developed—a major obstacle in the rapid development of Central Asia in general.

OIL AND NATURAL GAS

As was mentioned, oil and natural gas production represent Kazakhstan's main economic activity. Supported today by growing investment from multinational corporations and foreign governments, exploration for and production of these resources increased significantly during the past decade. Some $10 billion was invested in Kazakhstan's oil industry during 1992–2001. The government hopes to earn up to $70 billion in oil revenues, based mainly on foreign investments, during the next 25 years. Oil fields are mainly located in the western part of the country and offshore at the Caspian Sea. The largest fields are located in Tengiz, Karachaganak, and Kashagan. They account for a majority of (recoverable) reserves.

Exploration and Production

Oil exploration in the region is still in its initial phase. It is believed that vast stores of oil remain undiscovered in the region. The huge Kashagan oilfield may be the richest deposit of petroleum discovered in the past four decades. Additionally, recent research suggests that the huge Kashagan field may actually contain up to three times more petroleum than its current proven reserves. So far, Kazakhstan's proven oil reserves are between 5.5 to 17.5 billion barrels. That number, however, is subject to change. New reserves are being discovered each year.

Kazakhstan's oil production has risen by 60 percent since the early 1990s. There is a drastic difference, however, between petroleum production and domestic consumption. After independence, consumption within the country actually declined until 1997. Since then, domestic consumption has grown, but much slower than production. This is yet another sign that Kazakhstan desperately needs to further develop its domestic economy. Of the 800,000 barrels of oil produced daily in the country, only about 250,000 are consumed in Kazakhstan itself. The rest is exported. By 2010, the government plans to increase daily production to three billion barrels.

Theoretically, at least, Kazakhstan is one of the world's leading storehouses of natural gas reserves. Yet the country consumes three times more natural gas than it produces. To meet domestic demands, the country must import natural gas from its neighbors, mostly Russia and Uzbekistan. Much of the problem rests with the country's very poorly developed distribution network. Proven natural gas reserves amount to almost 79 trillion cubic feet, nearly half of which are in the Karachaganak field. And much more, no doubt, will be discovered.

Foreign Investments

Kazakhstan's government realizes that because of the high costs of petroleum research, exploration, and production, the country must cooperate with foreign companies. For this reason, the government favors a policy of establishing joint projects with foreign investors. Early in 2001, the government formed a national foundation for the purpose of cooperating with investors, regulating taxes, and allocating royalties provided from partners. Partners in different ventures and consortiums include almost all major oil suppliers in the world, ranging from the American ChevronTexaco to the British-American BPAmoco, Italian Agip, and the government of Oman.

Businesses from all over the world have made investments in Kazakhstan's natural resource industries. Among these corporations is American Chevron Texaco. These Kazakh girls are attending the opening ceremony of a new Texaco filling station.

If the country is to realize its full potential in oil and natural gas production, it needs to overcome two major obstacles. First, issues relating to political boundaries and national "ownership" of drilling and production rights in the Caspian Sea must be resolved. Second, the country lacks an well-integrated network of pipelines, a factor that limits both production and distribution. Countries that share an interest in offshore exploration (Kazakhstan, Russia, Turkmenistan, Iran, and Azerbaijan) still search for an agreement that will finally and fairly divide the Caspian Sea into five interest zones. Because of the huge reserves of oil and natural gas in the Caspian basin, each country wants to profit as much as possible by claming specific areas. When the same region was divided between the Soviet Union and Iran, both countries had a bilateral agreement. But in 1991, Kazakhstan, Turkmenistan, and Azerbaijan entered the fray as newly independent countries facing upon the Caspian. They wanted the have their fair share of the basin's vast wealth. This remains a very thorny, and still not fully resolved, issue. To date, Kazakhstan has had few problems with its neighbors Russia and Turkmenistan. If new offshore fields are discovered, however, conflicts could once again flare as a major political issue.

Problems with Distribution

As a landlocked country, Kazakhstan must have agreements other countries in order to export its energy surpluses. Most of the country's transportation networks were built during the Soviet era. They were designed primarily to serve the needs of several European Soviet republics, mainly Russia and Ukraine. Less consideration was given to adequately linking the cities and regions of Kazakhstan. For this reason, some of the country's urban areas remain quite isolated. For nearly a century, Russian interests focused more on Uzbekistan than on Kazakhstan. This is evident in the highway network. Today, major roads connect Uzbekistan's capital city, Tashkent, with

Russia via a route located in western Kazakhstan. But the western part of the country is not connected to the east and southeast, where most Kazakhs live. In the northern oblasts the situation is quite similar. There, in areas that were long dominated by Russian settlements, links to (now) Russia are much better than they are to southern Kazakhstan.

Poor transportation linkages create a number of problems for Kazakhstan. In such a huge land size adds to the cost of transport. Many areas remain quite isolated not only from the outside world, but from areas within the country itself. There are other costs to bear as well. For example, Kazakhs possess much more oil than they can consume. But oil refineries located in northern Kazakhstan must import oil from Russia. Transportation facilities are not in place to move petroleum from the country's areas of production in the south. To improve traffic within the southern oblasts, the government invested $185 million in railroad reconstruction. The improvement reduced the rail distance between northern and southern Kazakhstan by some 375 miles (600 kilometers).

Several hundred million dollars also have been invested in highway construction. The most recent project, costing $130 million, vastly improved the connection between the old capital, Almaty, and the new capital, Astana. Nearly all the country's transportation infrastructure is left over from the Soviet era, much of it being more than a half-century old. Highways and railroads are in desperate need of upgrading. Kazakhstan has approximately 11,200 miles (18,000 kilometers) of railroads, 52,600 miles (83,000 kilometers) of paved highways, and 2,500 miles (4,000 kilometers) of navigable waterways.

All oil export routes from Kazakhstan must pass through Russian territory. Theoretically, at least, this could pose a problem, because the major consumers of Caspian oil are Western European countries. Fortunately, Russia and Kazakhstan reached a joint agreement in May 2002 that will ensure a steady flow of Kazakh oil to the European market.

This arrangement allows Kazakhstan to transport its exported oil directly to international buyers. It also makes it possible for Turkmenistan's natural gas to be piped across Kazakhstan en route to markets. Because the Kazakh government receives royalties for the use of transcountry natural gas pipelines, it invested $170 million to upgrade the existing Soviet-built lines that were in very poor condition.

COAL, MINERALS, AND ELECTRICITY

The increase in the price of many minerals on the world market at the end of the 1990s boosted Kazakhstan's production and export of minerals and coal. After gaining its independence, Kazakhstan saw its mineral production decline by nearly 50 percent from 1991 to 1995. But the mining industry has since recovered, and today it exports more coal than any other former Soviet republic. Russia, the largest importer, also became financially involved in the development of some of Kazakhstan's mines.

Kazakhstan's network for distributing electricity suffers the same problems that affect its highways and railroads. The distribution system is very poorly integrated. Kazakhstan may be the only country in the world, in fact, that has an electrical energy grid that is divided in the following fashion: in the north, it is linked to Russia's network; in the south, it is connected to southern and central Asian countries. Even though current production is higher than domestic consumption, Kazakhstan needs to restructure and upgrade its existing network. Since 1999, some $140 million had been provided for network upgrade.

AGRICULTURE

In the 1950s, Soviet Communist Party General Secretary Nikita Khrushchev announced a very ambitious agricultural development program called the "Virgin Lands" project. The project focused primarily on Kazakhstan and, when implemented,

Although natural resources bring in the most money for Kazakhstan, agriculture remains a big part of the economy. Wheat, in particular, is a major crop. Before the fall of the Soviet Union in 1991, Kazakhstan's wheat fields, such as these in the nation's northern region, produced the third-largest amount of wheat of all the Soviet states.

was going to make the country a major agricultural producer. Over one-half of the land suitable for crop farming—approximately 25 million hectares, an area roughly the size of the state of Oregon—was cultivated. Before the collapse of the Soviet Union, Kazakhstan ranked third among the Soviet Republics in agricultural production. Today, grains, predominantly wheat, are being produced in northern oblasts. Cotton and rice account for most agricultural production in southern oblasts. Kazakhstan is, of course, a significant producer of meat. Most of its land is still used for livestock grazing.

Unfortunately, the agricultural adventures of the Soviet-era planners did not consider potential environmental problems. Irrigation techniques used in Soviet Central Asia resulted in serious damage to the Aral Sea, Syr Darya, and Lake Balkhash. Also, some experts believe that farming expanded too far on land poorly suited to raising crops. The result has been large-scale environmental degradation, particularly in the form of soil erosion.

With better organization, taxation, and governmental support, Kazakhstan could become one of the world's leading food producers. A rapid increase in the consumption of grain and meat in neighboring China may provide the needed stimulus for making the necessary changes. Shipping food-stuffs to China, whether grain or meat, would involve minimal transportation expenses. Today, agriculture contributes sig-nificantly to Kazakhstan's positive trade balance. With proper planning and support, agriculture production and the export of commodities should become an even greater contributor to the country's trade.

TRADE

Kazakhstan exports more than it imports. Primarily because of oil production and agriculture, a positive trade balance has been achieved ever since Kazakhstan stabilized its economy during the mid-1990s. The gross external debt, however, has increased from less than $10 billion (US) in 1998 to more than $12 billion in 2000. This indebtedness is of great concern to the government, because loans from international monetary institutions are desperately needed to further develop the country and its economy.

Cooperation with many foreign companies has already

been achieved. In 2001, more than 2,500 foreign companies were conducting business in Kazakhstan, either individually or as a part of a joint economic venture. Currently, Russia (with approximately 540 companies) and Turkey (with some 360) are the countries with the greatest number of companies involved in Kazakhstan. Inasmuch as Russia is Kazakhstan's leading trading partner, its position in this regard is not surprising. The United States, with approximately 200 companies involved in services, trade, and commerce in Kazakhstan, ranks third. Trade between the United States and Kazakhstan is increasing each year, however, and the trade balance between the countries is narrowing. In 2000, the trade balance was only $270–210 million in favor of the United States, compared with $350–380 million just one year earlier.

Seen here with its modern skyscrapers rising in the distance, the city of Astana became the capital of Kazakhstan in 1997. Although it was still a small population center with mud houses as recently as the 1950s, Astana was at one time the Soviet Union's choice for a new Kazakh capital. It was not until President Nursultan Nazarbayev took office, however, that the change of the capital from Almaty to Astana was actually made.

7

Cities and Regions

Kazakhstan can be divided into many different regions based on a variety of physical or cultural geographical patterns. This chapter tours Kazakhstan's 14 oblasts (administrative units similar to U.S. states) and the most important regional centers in each. It should be noted that the population and ethnic data for these regions and cities are difficult to determine. Many Europeans, particularly Russians and Germans, have left the area during the past decade. Figures pertaining to population and ethnic structure are based on the latest data available, from 1999.

ASTANA, THE NEW KAZAKH CAPITAL

Astana is Kazakhstan's newest capital city and the center of Akmola oblast. When the government transferred the administration from then-capital Almaty to central Kazakhstan's city of

Akmola, it changed the city's name. Astana means "the capital" in the Kazakh language. The official change took place on December 10, 1997, during the visit of high-ranking Russian officials. Kazakh President Nursultan Nazarbayev publicly explained that the primary reasons for moving the capital from Almaty to Akmola (Astana) were environmental, economic, and geographical. Most political geographers agree, however, that the real reasons for the change were strictly political.

Nazarbayev's publicly stated reasons included such factors as the seismic instability around Almaty. The region is prone to earthquakes, some of which can be extremely damaging. He also noted that the area of the old capital is very close to the Chinese border. He also claimed to seek a better balance in the distribution of the nation's economic prosperity; the Almaty region is the most prosperous in the country, whereas Akmola oblast is relatively poor. Scholars, on the other hand, believe that relocating the seat of government to a more central location was really a step to further establish Kazakhstan's independence from Russia. President Nazarbayev's real fear, they suggest, is that the northern provinces (oblasts) might attempt to secede from Kazakhstan.

After carefully waiting for several years, Nazarbayev implemented his bold decision to establish stronger control over the country by moving the capital. Until the 1950s, Astana was little more than a provincial town and service center similar to many towns established during tsarist Russia's expansion eastward in the nineteenth century. In that decade, Nikita Khrushchev, leader of the Soviet Union, announced his Virgin Lands program for agricultural development in northern Kazakhstan.

The region in which Astana is located was to be one of the centers of Khrushchev's ambitious plan. Astana's importance increased greatly, and, as the Soviets frequently did during the Communist era, they changed the town's name to

Tselinograd, which in Russian means "City of Virgin Lands." Between the 1960s and early 1990s, Tselinograd developed into a major Kazakhstan industrial and educational center. Different types of grain and dairy products became major branches of industry. Other important economic production included metallurgy and the manufacture of automobiles and construction materials.

After Kazakhstan gained its independence, the government once again changed the city's name (and many of the country's other toponyms, or place names, that had been changed by the Soviets) to Aqmola (Akmola is the Russian spelling, a reflection of the large number of ethnic Russians living in the region). Finally, five years later, the city changed its name once again, this time to Astana.

Although the past decade has witnessed a large emigration (out-migration) of Russians from Astana, the city's population continues to grow. Its current population of about 320,000 is expected to grow to more than 500,000 in the next 20 to 25 years. Recently, the government announced plans to improve the education and transportation systems in Astana and to improve the region's infrastructure. These and other changes resulting from the city's new role as capital should help trigger economic development and population growth.

ALMATY, THE OLD CAPITAL

Almaty, the previous capital of Kazakhstan and currently the center of Almaty oblast, was better known by its Russian name Alma-Ata, which means the "father of apples." Astana and Almaty share some similarities, including their origin, a high proportion of ethnic Russians in their population, and official names that changed with changing political regimes. Modern Almaty grew from a fort built by the Russian military in 1854. A previous settlement had existed at the site since ancient times. Its original name was Vernyi, which was changed in 1921 to Alma-Ata after the Russian Revolution. When

The previous capital of Kazakhstan was Almaty, an ancient settlement that eventually grew into the sprawling modern city seen here. As one of the main population centers of Central Asia, Almaty has more than a million residents.

Kazakhstan achieved independence, the city was officially renamed Almaty, the Kazakh version.

Through the decades, Almaty developed into a modern city with over one million inhabitants. It became one of the major centers in Soviet Central Asia and, perhaps, one of the most beautifully located cities in the region. The towering, snow-capped peaks of the Tian Shan range dominate the local landscape. The region is now becoming a popular tourist destination.

Travelers who find their way to Almaty immediately notice its natural beauty and the fascinating culture of the local residents. Numerous parks dot the urban landscape, and works of art, particularly in the form of sculptures, can be seen throughout much of the city. During the 1990s, Almaty became more accessible to outside travelers. They, in turn, helped the residents of Almaty develop a more cosmopolitan (some would say "worldly") outlook. The city's geographical location is 2,000 feet (610 meters) above sea level at a point where the rolling plains and steppe grasslands blend into mountains. But, as already mentioned, it is also a zone of seismic activity. Strong earthquakes in 1887 and 1911 severely damaged the city.

After the earthquakes, Almaty was rebuilt into the industrial, educational, and cultural center of Kazakhstan. Locals are employed in various industries, from heavy machinery and metallurgy to lumber production. Institutions of higher learning and the Academy of Science (founded in 1946) are based in Almaty, as is the Puskhin Library, with over five million books and documents and an impressive collection of Asian manuscripts.

During the Soviet era, sports and recreation were of special importance here. The city is home to some famous winter sport facilities, including the world-class ice skating stadium, a facility that hosts many international events.

KAZAKHSTAN'S PROVINCES AND OTHER CITIES

Karaganda oblast is the heart of Kazakhstan's most important mining region. Some of the country's largest mines are located in this province that is home to some 1.5 million people. In 1999, the ethnic structure was almost equally divided among Russians and Kazakhs. Karaganda oblast got its name from the town of the same name that was built in the middle of the nineteenth century as a coal mining center. The city of Karaganda grew to become the second-largest urban center in the country with around 450,000 inhabitants. Industrial development and the emergence of surrounding mining settlements spurred the rapid urban growth that has occurred there since the 1930s.

Today, Karaganda also is the administrative and educational center of the oblast. It is home to the provincial capital, and also has both university, polytechnic, and medical institutes. The city also operates the only German-language theater in Central Asia. The space center Baikonur, near the town of Leninsk, is located in the western portion of Karaganda oblast. It was the most important space center in the Soviet Union. Yuri Gagarin, the first man in space, launched his trip from Baikonur. Today, Russia leases a space center from Kazakhstan for $125 million.

Shymkent has a somewhat different history than do the previously mentioned cities. Its importance reaches back many centuries. Located close to the border with Uzbekistan, Shymkent was an important early administrative and economic center. The city, located on caravan trade routes, was already an important settlement long before the Russians came to the region.

Since the twelfth century, when it was first built, Shymkent served as a fort for local khaganates. In 1864, the city was occupied by Russian forces and became part of the Russian Empire. During the next 150 years it would become a modern city with over 350,000 inhabitants. Today, it is the third-largest urban center in Kazakhstan.

One factor contributing to the city's development is its location on a major railroad that connects the Siberian provinces and with the Central Asian countries of Uzbekistan and Turkmenistan. Development of a mining industry also contributed to Shymkent's growth and its large number of Russian and other European residents. It was one of the

Kazakhstan is home to the Khrunichev Space Center, which was a very important part of the Soviet Union's scientific community. This rocket-booster is seen during preparations for a 2001 space mission launch from Khrunichev.

USSR's leading lead and zinc producers. Unfortunately, industry also was responsible for extensive environmental pollution. And since independence, the region's economy has suffered a decline resulting in a very high unemployment rate. Shymkent also has, among other attractions, museums and research institutes dedicated to the famous Karakul sheep that originated in the region.

Taraz is located in south-central Kazakhstan. The city,

also with about 350,000 inhabitants, is the capital and largest city of Zhambyl oblast. Its history and function is not much different than that of neighboring Shymkent. Taraz appeared in history around the sixth century as one of the towns on the Silk Road between China and Europe. Since then, it changed rulers on numerous occasions until the Russians took over in 1864 and, as they did with other regional centers, renamed it Aulie-Ata. During the twentieth century, the importance of Taraz increased since it was located on the previously mentioned railroad linking Siberia with Uzbekistan and Turkmenistan.

Between 1938 and 1997, Taraz experienced another name change, to Dzhambul, but in January 1997 the government decided to change it back. Dzhambul was the name of a famous Kazakh poet. Although Taraz is today mainly an industrial city with heavy air pollution and other environmental problems, it also has some interesting cultural landmarks. There are several different millennium-old mausoleums that show the preserved heritage of Central Asia.

East Kazakhstan oblast has two important cities, both of which are located on the Irtysh River. *Ust-Kamenogorsk*, settled as a Russian outpost in 1720, is the oblast capital. The second city, *Semipalatinsk (Semey)*, also was settled as a Russian outpost in 1718. Both communities first served as strategic fortified trading posts between the Russian Empire and China. Since the nineteenth century the region has gained importance as a mining center, particularly for its rich deposits of gold.

Both cities have around 300,000 inhabitants, many of whom represent the leading industrial, cultural, and educational leaders of East Kazakhstan. Until the 1990s the Russian ethnic group represented the majority. During recent years, however, many Russians have left the region and the number of ethnic Kazakhs has increased, especially in Semipalatinsk. The infamous Soviet nuclear testing center was located not far from the city. Even though nuclear testing was discontinued, citizens continue to pay a high price as a result of the pollution from the testing. The incidence of certain types of cancer and other dangerous illnesses is very high here.

The *Pavlodar* oblast borders Siberia. Ethnically, the oblast has a population that is almost equally divided between Russians and Kazakhs. It also is the site of considerable economic development and future potential. The oblast borders Russian Siberia and owes much of its development to geographic location and the natural environment. The capital of the Pavlodar oblast also is Pavlodar, a city of about 300,000. Although it was founded in 1720 as yet another Russian fort, the settlement did not develop into a large city until the twentieth century. During the Soviet era, Pavlodar underwent rapid industrial development and economic growth that stimulated immigration. The landscape is dominantly Russian. In fact, the city still has a considerable amount of Soviet iconography (images), including a statue of Lenin. In 1978, a large oil refinery was built, creating many new jobs. Development slowed drastically during the 1990s, however, resulting in many factories closing their doors and rising unemployment.

The North Kazakhstan oblast's capital is *Petropavlovsk*. It was founded in 1752 as another in a long line of Russian military stations. For nearly 150 years, the town was of little significance. Then, in 1896, the Trans-Siberian railway that connects Moscow and the Far East port of Vladivostok reached Petropavlovsk. With the arrival of the railroad, the city's importance increased immediately. It soon grew into the most important and modern center of North Kazakhstan, known for its gold mining as well as its railroad link. Today, Petropavlovsk is a thriving city of over 200,000.

Northwestern Kazakhstan's oblasts experienced rapid economic development in the decades following the beginning of Khrushchev's Virgin Lands agricultural development project. The oblast of *Kostanay,* and its capital city of the same name (population 230,000), owe much of their progress to

Khrushchev's plan. In addition to being a center of agricultural production, the oblast has important railway connections and large iron deposits in the local steppes around Rudnyi.

Founded in 1869, *Aktobe* grew to become the capital of the *Aktiubinsk* oblast that also is situated in northwestern Kazakhstan. Today Aktobe has 260,000 inhabitants. Major industries of Aktiubinsk oblast are chromium and machinery products.

The most western oblast, as it name says, is West Kazakhstan. Its capital, *Uralsk* (population 200,000), is located where the steppes touch the right bank (western shore) of the Ural River that flows from the Ural Mountains to the Caspian Sea. It is one of the oldest Russian-built cities in Kazakhstan and Russian influence can be seen everywhere. The city also is host of the oldest theater in Kazakhstan. At the beginning of the seventeenth century, groups of Cossacks moved into the area and settled. Traditionally, West Kazakhstan's economy has been based on agricultural production. Recently, however, the discovery of large oil deposits in Karachaganak have given a huge boost to the region's importance.

Atyrau is potentially the richest oblast in Kazakhstan. It covers a large area bordering the northeastern part of the Caspian Sea. Huge deposits of oil and natural gas are located both offshore (the Kashgan field) and onshore (near the city of Tengiz) as well. The city of *Atyrau* (population 150,000) was built in the seventeenth century. Its primary early function was as a fishing village on the Caspian Sea. Until 1992, the city was named Guryev in honor of Mikhail Guryev, the person who first established a permanent settlement at the site. Although fishing and fish processing continue to contribute to the city's economy, the oil industry is now the most important economic activity.

Aktau, a city also of 150,000 inhabitants, is best known for fishing and the production of high-quality Caspian caviar (sturgeon eggs). The city is the capital of *Mangistau* oblast, which also has deposits of oil. Some of the major oil drilling locations are near Uzen and Tenge.

Finally, *Kyzyl-Orda* (population 160,000) is a capital of the oblast that bears the same name. This south-central Kazakh city, located east of the Aral Sea, is one of the country's former capitals. From 1925 to 1929, Kyzyl-Orda was the capital of the Kazakhstan Soviet Republic, before the seat of government was moved to Almaty. The oblast is less developed economically than most others. Water from the Syr Darya supports irrigated agriculture, primarily of cotton. And oil deposits have been found near Kumkol, about 100 miles (160 kilometers) north of Kyzyl-Orda.

Since achieving independence from the Soviet Union in 1991, the people of Kazakhstan have worked hard to establish their national identity. Although they have faced some problems, they remain optimistic, as is evident in this painting done by Kazakh children. It shows a cheerful, vibrant land decorated with people, animals, and flowers.

CHAPTER 8

The Future of Kazakhstan

The main question for both Kazakhs and the international community concerning Kazakhstan's future is whether the country will achieve economic prosperity in the coming decades. Particularly with its enormous oil and natural gas resources, the country has tremendous potential for economic development. Theoretically, at least, Kazakhstan could become one of Asia's leading economic powers. The country also could become the most economically advanced among the now independent countries that formerly were republics within the Soviet Union.

Only the people of Kazakhstan have the power to determine their future. Under Soviet control, the Kazakhs spent seven decades under one-party Communist rule. In 1990, when a multiparty democracy was introduced, Kazakhs chose their current president to lead them into the twenty-first century. Tired of Moscow's political domination, they elected their own man, a former Communist,

Nursultan Nazarbayev, who, more than a decade later, still serves as president.

Opposition to the present government is practically nonexistent, however, since it would not be tolerated. This situation in Kazakhstan is something that has occurred in nearly all former Soviet republics. Before elections, country leaders promised the separation of powers and the establishment of an American type of democracy. Once the former Communist Party members achieved victory, however, things changed rapidly. They concentrated on introducing constitutional changes by "popular" referendum that expanded presidential powers and limited the power of the legislature (parliament). Once they gained additional constitutional power by reducing checks-and-balances by other branches of government, they began to silence other political parties or watchdog groups. At the same time, the families of those in power often became involved in extensive corruption and various scandals. In Kazakhstan, for example, the president has been unable to explain (in a satisfactory manner) the source of the funds in an $80 million account in a Swiss bank with which he is connected.

Corruption on all levels of government—from local politicians to the highest circles of power—is an everyday occurrence in postcommunist countries. But there are other Communist-era related problems as well. Communist governments centrally planned their countries' economies. This resulted in the newly emerged independent former Soviet republics having inadequate networks of highways, railroads, and other vital aspects of infrastructure, such as power lines and pipelines. Also, with so much of the country's capital resources being siphoned off by government leaders, few funds are available to upgrade the infrastructure to Western levels.

Kazakhs must understand that only radical changes in some elements of their lifestyle can bring them wanted prosperity. One of these elements is the elimination of the growing apathy toward political participation among the Kazakhstan's population. To change the political conditions and create a different climate, voters' active engagement is necessary.

There is another important emotional issue that must be resolved among Kazakhs: they must begin concentrating on the future, rather than reliving the past. Even to an outsider, it is obvious that many ethnic Kazakhs and ethnic Russians still have the burden of the Soviet Union on their minds. To Kazakhs, Russia represents another form of imperialistic force that ruled their homelands for many decades. Governmental policies during the 1990s proved that Kazakhs desperately want to establish their independence from Russia in all possible ways. At the same time, a vast number of Kazakhstan's Russians did not want to accept the fact that they were now living in a different country. The first step toward joint life in Kazakhstan should be the formation of a bilingual society where the majority of people speak both the Kazakh and Russian languages. By knowing and understanding different cultures, we develop respect toward them; rejection almost always is a product of ignorance. As a result of prejudice and discrimination exhibited by both Russians and Kazakhs, several million Russians left Kazakhstan between 1991 and 2002. A great number of them were well-educated people, thereby creating a "brain drain" that deprived the country of some of its best human resources.

As we know, people are a country's most important capital. Educated, hard-working people are essential to the economic development of any nation. The Kazakhs waited for so long to have a country of their own. Now that they have achieved their precious independence, they must make the most of the opportunity.

Part of Kazakhstan's future is located deep below the surface. Proven oil and natural gas reserves in the country's western oblasts are enormous. Western multinational companies are more than willing to cooperate with Kazakhs and establish joint ventures for further research and exploration. It can bring thousands of new jobs to young people and lower the high unemployment rate in Kazakhstan.

Few Americans consider themselves to be experts in the physical, historical, and cultural geography of the former Soviet Union. Kazakhstan, to many people, is little more than one of the region's many "stan"-ending countries in which some type of conflict is occurring. Certainly the country is not a primary tourist destination. Most people simply do not know much about Central Asia.

Yet Kazakhstan is a peaceful and life-loving country that has much to offer. Kazakhs should invite outsiders to visit and enjoy their country more often. They need to show others that their country is more than just a former nuclear testing range, a space center, or oil fields. It is a country with much to recommend it to the visitor in search of an interesting and unique culture and destination.

Country Name	Conventional long form: Republic of Kazakhstan Conventional short form: Kazakhstan
Capital	Astana
Population	16,741,519 (2002 est.)
Area	Total: 1,688,530 sq mi (2,717,300 sq km) Land: 1,659,013 sq mi (2,669,800 sq km) Water: 29,516 sq mi (47,500 sq km)
Land Boundaries	Total: 7,646 mi (12,012 km)
Border Countries	China, 952 mi (1,533 km border), Kyrgyzstan, 653 mi (1,051 km border), Russia, 4,255 mi (6,846 km border), Turkmenistan, 235 mi (379 km border), Uzbekistan, 1,368 mi (2,203 km border)
Climate	Continental, cold winters and hot summers, arid, and semiarid
Highest Point	Khan Tangiri Shyngy (Pik Khan-Tengri), 6,995 m
Life Expectancy	Total population: 63.29 years Male: 57.87 years Female: 68.97 years (2001 est.)
Literacy	Definition: age 15 and over can read and write Total of Population: 98%
Ethnic Groups	Kazakh (Qazaq) 53.4%, Russian 30%, Ukrainian 3.7%, Uzbek 2.5%, German 2.4%, Uighur 1.4%, other 6.6%
Religions	Muslim 47%, Russian Orthodox 44%, Protestant 2%, other 7%
Independence	December 16, 1991
GDP Purchasing Power Parity (PPP)	$85.6 billion (2000 est.)
GDP per Capita	$5,000 (2000 est.)
Industries	Oil, coal, iron ore, manganese, chromite, lead, zinc, copper, titanium, bauxite, gold, silver, phosphates, sulfur, iron and steel, nonferrous metal, tractors and other agricultural machinery, electric motors, construction materials.
Exports	Commodities: oil 40%, ferrous and nonferrous metals, machinery, chemicals, grain, wool, meat, coal.
Exports	Partners: European Union 23%, Russia 20%, China 8% (1999)
Imports	Commodities: machinery and parts, industrial materials, oil and gas, vehicles.
Imports	Partners: Russia 37%, U.S., Uzbekistan, Turkey, U.K., Germany, Ukraine, South Korea (1999)

History at a Glance

1916	Riots against Tsarist rule.
1917	Short-term semi-independence of Kazakhstan.
1920–1925	Under the name of Kirghiz ASSR, Kazakhstan is autonomous region in the Soviet Union.
1936	Formation of Kazakhstan Soviet Republic; exists until 1991.
1991	Kazakhstan proclaims independence from the Soviet Union; last former Soviet republic to do so.
1991	First democratic elections. Nursultan Nazarbayev becomes president.
1993 and 1995	Constitutional changes further expand presidential power and limit power of legislative branch.
1999	President Nazarbayev reelected.

Further Reading

Akiner, Shirin. *The Formation of Kazakh Identity: From Tribe to Nation-State.* London: Royal Institute of International Affairs, Russian and CIS Programme, 1995.

Bradley, Catherine. *Kazakhstan.* Brookfield, CT: Millbrook Press, 1993.

Central Intelligence Agency (U.S.). *CIA — The World Factbook: Kazakhstan. http://www.cia.gov/cia/publications/factbook/* (current).

Eastep, Wayne, et. al. *The Soul of Kazakhstan.* New York: Easton Press, 2001.

Olcott, Martha Brill. *The Kazakhs.* Stanford, CA: Hoover Institution Press, Stanford University, 1987.

Official Kazakhstan. The official site of the President of the Republic of Kazakhstan at *http://www.president.kz.*

Paksoy, H.B. (ed.). *Central Asia reader: the rediscover of history.* Armonk, N.Y.: M.E. Sharpe, 1994.

Pang, Guek-Cheng. *Kazakhstan.* New York: Marshall Cavendish, 2001.

Svanberg, Ingvar (ed.). *Contemporary Kazaks: Cultural and Social Perspectives.* New York: St. Martin's Press, 1999.

Thomas, Paul. *The Central Asian States — Tajikstan, Uzbekistan, Kyrgyzstan, Turkmenistan.* Brookfield, CT: Millbrook Press, 1992.

Index

Index

Index

About the Author

ZORAN "ZOK" PAVLOVIĆ is a professional geographer who resides and works in Brookings, South Dakota. His previous contributions to the Chelsea House Major World Nations Series were *The Republic of Georgia* (with Charles F. "Fritz" Gritzner) and *Croatia*. When not studying and writing, Zok enjoys traveling with his wife, Erin, and sharing a glass of red wine with his friend and fellow connoisseur Fritz Gritzner.

CHARLES F. ("FRITZ") GRITZNER is Distinguished Professor of Geography at South Dakota University in Brookings. He is now in his fifth decade of college teaching and research. During his career, he has taught more than 60 different courses, spanning the fields of physical, cultural, and regional geography. In addition to his teaching, he enjoys writing, working with teachers, and sharing his love for geography with students. As consulting editor for the MODERN WORLD NATIONS series, he has a wonderful opportunity to combine each of these "hobbies." Fritz has served as both president and executive director of the National Council for Geographic Education and has received the Council's highest honor, the George J. Miller Award for Distinguished Service.

Picture Credits

page

8: New Millennium Images	56: New Millennium Images
12: 21st Century Publishing	58: Kuznetcov Nikolay/Itar-Tass/NMI
14: New Millennium Images	62: Yuri Kochetkov/AFP/NMI
18: 21st Century Publishing	66: Antoly Ustinenko/Itar-Tass/NMI
23: New Millennium Images	70; Bruce Stanley/AP
28: NASA/AFP/NMI	75: Shamil Zhumatov/Reuters/NMI
30: New Millennium Images	79: New Millennium Images
40: Ustinenko Anatoly/Itar-Tass/NMI	82: Malyshev/Itar-Tass/NMI
43: Shamil Zhumatov/Reuters/NMI	86: New Millennium Images
46: Antoly Ustinenko/Itar-Tass/NMI	89: Kazak Sergei/Itar-Tass/NMI
53: Kuznetcov Nikolay/Itar-Tass/NMI	94: Kuznetcov Nikolay/Itar-Tass/NMI

Cover: Shamil Zhumatov/Reuters/NMI